Collection Development in the Electronic Environment: Shifting Priorities

Collection Development in the Electronic Environment: Shifting Priorities has been co-published simultaneously as *Journal of Library Administration,* Volume 28, Number 4 1999.

The *Journal of Library Administration* Monographic "Separates"

Below is a list of "separates," which in serials librarianship means a special issue simultaneously published as a special journal issue or double-issue *and* as a "separate" hardbound monograph. (This is a format which we also call a "DocuSerial.")

"Separates" are published because specialized libraries or professionals may wish to purchase a specific thematic issue by itself in a format which can be separately cataloged and shelved, as opposed to purchasing the journal on an on-going basis. Faculty members may also more easily consider a "separate" for classroom adoption.

"Separates" are carefully classified separately with the major book jobbers so that the journal tie-in can be noted on new book order slips to avoid duplicate purchasing.

You may wish to visit Haworth's Website at . . .

http://www.haworthpressinc.com

. . . to search our online catalog for complete tables of contents of these separates and related publications.

You may also call 1-800-HAWORTH (outside US/Canada: 607-722-5857), or Fax 1-800-895-0582 (outside US/Canada: 607-771-0012), or e-mail at:

getinfo@haworthpressinc.com

Collection Development in the Electronic Environment: Shifting Priorities, edited by Sul H. Lee (Vol. 28, No. 4, 1999). *Through case studies and firsthand experiences, this volume discusses meeting the needs of scholars at universities, budgeting issues, user education, staffing in the electronic age, collaborating libraries and resources, and how vendors meet the needs of different customers.*

The Age Demographics of Academic Librarians: A Profession Apart, by Stanley J. Wilder (Vol. 28, No. 3, 1999). *The average age of librarians has been increasing dramatically since 1990. This unique book will provide insights on how this demographic issue can impact a library and what can be done to make the effects positive.*

Collection Development in a Digital Environment, edited by Sul H. Lee (Vol. 28, No. 1, 1999). *Explores ethical and technological dilemmas of collection development and gives several suggestions on how a library can successfully deal with these challenges and provide patrons with the information they need.*

Scholarship, Research Libraries, and Global Publishing, by Jutta Reed-Scott (Vol. 27, No. 3/4, 1999). *This book documents a research project in conjunction with the Association of Research Libraries (ARL) that explores the issue of foreign acquisition and how it affects collection in international studies, area studies, collection development, and practices of international research libraries.*

Managing Multicultural Diversity in the Library: Principles and Issues for Administrators, edited by Mark Winston (Vol. 27, No. 1/2, 1999). *Defines diversity, clarifies why it is important to address issues of diversity; and identifies goals related to diversity and how to go about achieving those goals.*

Information Technology Planing, edited by Lori A. Goetsch (Vol. 26, No. 3/4, 1999). *Offers innovative approaches and strategies useful in your library and provides some food for thought about information technology as we approach the millennium.*

The Economics of Information in the Networked Environment, edited by Meredith A. Butler, MLS, and Bruce R. Kingma, PhD (Vol. 26, No. 1/2, 1998). *"A book that should be read both by information professionals and by administrators, faculty and others who share a collective concern to provide the most information to the greatest number at the lowest cost in the networked environment."* (Thomas J. Galvin, PhD, Professor of Information Science and Policy, University at Albany, State University of New York)

OCLC 1967-1997: Thirty Years of Furthering Access to the World's Information, edited by K. Wayne Smith (Vol. 25, No. 2/3/4, 1998). *"A rich–and poignantly personal, at times–historical account of what is surely one of this century's most important developments in librarianship."* (Deanna B. Marcum, PhD, President, Council on Library and Information Resources, Washington, DC)

Management of Library and Archival Security: From the Outside Looking In, edited by Robert K. O'Neill, PhD (Vol. 25, No. 1, 1998). *"Provides useful advice and on-target insights for professionals caring for valuable documents and artifacts."* (Menzi L Behrnd-Klodt, JD, Attorney/Archivist, Klodt and Associates, Madison, WI)

Economics of Digital Information: Collection, Storage, and Delivery, edited by Sul H. Lee (Vol. 24, No. 4, 1997). *Highlights key concepts and issues vital to a library's successful venture into the digital environment and helps you understand why the transition from the printed page to the digital packet has been problematic for both creators of proprietary materials and users of those materials.*

The Academic Library Director: Reflections on a Position in Transition, edited by Frank D'Andraia, MLS (Vol. 24, No. 3, 1997). *"A useful collection to have whether you are seeking a position as director or conducting a search for one."* (College & Research Libraries News)

Emerging Patterns of Collection Development in Expanding Resource Sharing, Electronic Information, and Network Environment, edited by Sul H. Lee (Vol. 24, No. 1/2, 1997). *"The issues it deals with are common to us all. We all need to make our finds go further and our resources work harder, and there are ideas here which we can all develop."* (The Library Association Record)

Interlibrary Loan/Document Delivery and Customer Satisfaction: Strategies for Redesigning Services, edited by Pat L. Weaver-Meyers, Wilbur A. Stolt, Yem S. Fong (Vol. 23, No. 1/2, 1997). *"No interlibrary loan department supervisor at any mid-sized to large college or university library can afford not to read this book."* (Gregg Sapp, MLS, MEd, Head of Access Services, University of Miami, Richter Library, Coral Gables, Florida)

Access, Resource Sharing and Collection Development, edited by Sul H. Lee (Vol. 22, No. 4, 1996). *Features continuing investigation and discussion of important library issues, specifically the role of libraries in acquiring, storing, and disseminating information in different formats.*

Managing Change in Academic Libraries, edited by Joseph J. Branin (Vol. 22, No. 2/3, 1996). *"Touches on several aspects of academic library management, emphasizing the changes that are occurring at the present time. . . . Recommended this title for individuals or libraries interested in management aspects of academic libraries."* (RQ American Library Association)

Libraries and Student Assistants: Critical Links, edited by William K. Black, MLS (Vol. 21, No. 3/4, 1995). *"A handy reference work on many important aspects of managing student assistants. . . . Solid, useful information on basic management issues in this work and several chapters are useful for experienced managers."* (The Journal of Academic Librarianship)

The Future of Resource Sharing, edited by Shirley K. Baker and Mary E. Jackson, MLS (Vol. 21, No. 1/2, 1995). *"Recommended for library and information science schools because of its balanced presentation of the ILL/document delivery issues."* (Library Acquisitions: Practice and Theory)

The Future of Information Services, edited by Virginia Steel, MA, and C. Brigid Welch, MLS (Vol. 20, No. 3/4, 1995). *"The leadership discussions will be useful for library managers as will the discussions of how library structures and services might work in the next century."* (Australian Special Libraries)

The Dynamic Library Organizations in a Changing Environment, edited by Joan Giesecke, MLS, DPA (Vol. 20, No. 2, 1995). *"Provides a significant look at potential changes in the library* *world and presents its readers with possible ways to address the negative results of such changes. . . . Covers the key issues facing today's libraries. . . Two thumbs up!" (Marketing Library Resources)*

Access, Ownership, and Resource Sharing, edited by Sul H. Lee, PhD (Vol. 20, No. 1, 1995). *The contributing authors present a useful and informative look at the current status of information provision and some of the challenges the subject presents.*

Planning for Library Services: A Guide to Utilizing Planning Methods for Library Management, edited by Charles R. McClure, PhD (Vol. 2, No. 3/4, 1982). *"Should be read by anyone who is involved in planning processes of libraries–certainly by every administrator of a library or system." (American Reference Books Annual)*

Libraries as User-Centered Organizations: Imperatives for Organizational Change, edited by Meredith A. Butler (Vol. 19, No. 3/4, 1994). *"Presents a very timely and well-organized discussion of major trends and influences causing organizational changes." (Science Books & Films)*

Declining Acquisitions Budgets: Allocation, Collection Development and Impact Communication, edited by Sul H. Lee (Vol. 19, No. 2, 1994). *"Expert and provocative. . . . Presents many ways of looking at library budget deterioration and responses to it . . . There is much food for thought here. "(Library Resources & Technical Services)*

The Role and Future of Special Collections in Research Libraries: British and American Perspectives, edited by Sul H. Lee (Vol. 19, No. 1, 1993). *"A provocative but informative read for library users, academic administrators, and private sponsors." (International Journal of Information and Library Research)*

Catalysts for Change: Managing Libraries in the 1990s, edited by Gisela M. von Dran, DPA, MLS, and Jennifer Cargill, MSLS, MSed (Vol. 18, No. 3/4, 1994). *"A useful collection of articles which focuses on the need for librarians to employ enlightened management practices in order to adapt to, and thrive, in the rapidly changing information environment." (Australian Library Review)*

Integrating Total Quality Management in a Library Setting, edited by Susan Jurow, MLS, and Susan B. Barnard, MLS (Vol. 18, No. 1/2, 1993). *"Especially valuable are the librarian experiences that directly relate to real concerns about TQM. Recommended for all professional reading collections." (Library Journal)*

Leadership in Academic Libraries: Proceedings of the W. Porter Kellam Conference, The University of Georgia, May 7, 1991, edited by William Gray Potter (Vol. 17, No. 4, 1993). *"Will be of interest to those concerned with the history of American academic libraries." (Australian Library Review)*

Collection Assessment and Acquisitions Budgets, edited by Sul H. Lee (Vol. 17, No. 2, 1993). *Contains timely information about the assessment of academic library collections and the relationship of collection assessment to acquisition budgets.*

Developing Library Staff for the 21st Century, edited by Maureen Sullivan (Vol. 17, No. 1, 1992). *"I found myself enthralled with this highly readable publication. It is one of those rare compilations that manages to successfully integrate current general management operational thinking in the context of academic library management." (Bimonthly Review of Law Books)*

Vendor Evaluation and Acquisition Budgets, edited by Sul H. Lee (Vol. 16, No. 3, 1992). *"The title doesn't do justice to the true scope of this excellent collection of papers delivered at the sixth annual conference on library acquisitions sponsored by the University of Oklahoma Libraries." (Kent K. Hendrickson, BS, MALS, Dean of Libraries, University of Nebraska-Lincoln) Find insight discussions on the impact of rising costs on library budgets and management in this groundbreaking book.*

The Management of Library and Information Studies Education, edited by Herman L. Totten, PhD, MLS (Vol. 16 No. 1/2, 1992). *"Offers something of interest to everyone connected with*

LIS education–the undergraduate contemplating a master's degree, the doctoral student struggling with courses and career choices, the new faculty member aghast at conflicting responsibilities, the experienced but stressed LIS professor, and directors of LIS Schools." (Education Libraries)

Library Management in the Information Technology Environment: Issues, Policies, and Practice for Administrators, edited by Brice G. Hobrock, PhD, MLS (Vol. 15, No. 3/4, 1992). *"A road map to identify some of the alternative routes to the electronic library." (Stephen Rollins, Associate Dean for Library Services, General library, University of New Mexico)*

Managing Technical Services in the 90's, edited by Drew Racine (Vol. 15, No. 1/2, 1991). *"Presents an eclectic overview of the challenges currently facing all library technical services efforts. . . . Recommended to library administrators and interested practitioners." (Library Journal)*

Budgets for Acquisitions: Strategies for Serials, Monographs, and Electronic Formats, edited by Sul Lee (Vol. 14, No. 3, 1991). *"Much more than a series of handy tips for the careful shopper. This [book] is a most useful one–well-informed, thought-provoking, and authoritative." (Australian Library Review)*

Creative Planning for Library Administration: Leadership for the Future, edited by Kent Hendrickson, MALS (Vol. 14, No. 2, 1991). *"Provides some essential information on the planning process, and the mix of opinions and methodologies, as well as examples relevant to every library manager, resulting in a very readable foray into a topic too long avoided by many of us." (Canadian Library Journal)*

Strategic Planning in Higher Education: Implementing New Roles for the Academic Library, edited by James F. Williams, II, MLS (Vol. 13, No. 3/4, 1991). *"A welcome addition to the sparse literature on strategic planning in university libraries. Academic librarians considering strategic planning for their libraries will learn a great deal from this work." (Canadian Library Journal)*

Personnel Administration in an Automated Environment, edited by Philip E. Leinbach, MLS (Vol. 13 No. 1/2, 1990). *"An interesting and worthwhile volume, recommended to university library administrators and to others interested in thought-provoking discussion of the personnel implications of automation." (Canadian Library Journal)*

Library Development: A Future Imperative, edited by Dwight F. Burlingame, PhD (Vol. 12, No. 4, 1990). *"This volume provides an excellent overview of fundraising with special application to libraries. . . . A useful book that is highly recommended for all libraries." (Library Journal)*

Library Material Costs and Access to Information, edited by Sul Lee (Vol. 12, No. 3, 1991). *"A cohesive treatment of the issue. Although the book's contributors possess a research library perspective, the data and the ideas presented are of interest and benefit to the entire profession, especially academic librarians." (Library Resources and Technical Services)*

Training Issues and Strategies in Libraries, edited by Paul M. Gherman, MALS, and Frances O. Painter, MLS, MBA (Vol. 12, No. 2, 1990). *"There are . . . useful chapters, all by different authors, each with a preliminary summary of the content–a device that saves much time in deciding whether to read the whole chapter or merely skim through it. Many of the chapters are essentially practical without too much emphasis on theory. This book is a good investment." (Library Association Record)*

Library Education and Employer Expectations, edited by E. Dale Cluff, PhD, MLS (Vol. 11, No. 3/4, 1990). *"Useful to library school students and faculty interested in employment problems and employer perspectives. Librarians concerned with recruitment practices will also be interested." (Information Technology and Libraries)*

Managing Public Libraries in the 21st Century, edited by Pat Woodrum, MLS (Vol. 11, No. 1/2, 1989). *"A broad-based collection of topics that explores the management problems and possibilities public libraries will be facing in the 21st century. "(Robert Swisher, PhD, Director, School of Library and Information Studies, The University of Oklahoma)*

Human Resources Management in Libraries, edited by Gisela M. Webb, MLS, MPA (Vol. 10, No. 4, 1989). *"Thought provoking and enjoyable reading. . . . Provides valuable insights for the effective information manager." (Special Libraries)*

Creativity, Innovation, and Entrepreneurship in Libraries, edited by Donald E. Riggs, EdD, MLS (Vol. 10, No. 2/3, 1989). *"The volume is well worth reading as a whole. . . . There is very little repetition, and it should stimulate thought." (Australian Library Review)*

The Impact of Rising Costs of Serials and Monographs on Library Services and Programs, edited by Sul H. Lee (Vol. 10, No. 1, 1989). *". . . Sul Lee hit a winner here." (Serials Review)*

Computing, Electronic Publishing, and Information Technology: Their Impact on Academic Libraries, edited by Robin N. Downes (Vol. 9, No. 4, 1989). *"For a relatively short and easily digestible discussion of these issues this book can be recommended, not only to those in academic libraries, but also to those in similar types of library or information unit, and to academics and educators in the field." (Journal of Documentation)*

Library Management and Technical Services: The Changing Role of Technical Services in Library Organizations, edited by Jennifer Cargill, MSLS, MSed (Vol. 9, No. 1, 1988). *"As a practical and instructive guide to issues such as automation, personnel matters, education, management techniques and liaison with other services, senior library managers with a sincere interest in evaluating the role of their technical services should find this a timely publication." (Library Association Record)*

Management Issues in the Networking Environment, edited by Edward R. Johnson, PhD (Vol. 8, No. 3/4, 1989). *"Particularly useful for librarians/information specialists contemplating establishing a local network." (Australian Library Review)*

Acquisitions, Budgets, and Material Costs: Issues and Approaches, edited by Sul H. Lee (Supp. #2, 1988). *"The advice of these library practitioners is sensible and their insights illuminating for librarians in academic libraries." (American Reference Books Annual)*

Pricing and Costs of Monographs and Serials: National and International Issues, edited by Sul H. Lee (Supp. #l, 1987). *"Eminently readable. There is a good balance of chapters on serials and monographs and the perspective of suppliers, publishers, and library practitioners are presented. A book well worth reading." (Australasian College Libraries)*

Legal Issues for Library and Information Managers, edited by William Z. Nasri, JD, PhD (Vol. 7, No. 4, 1987). *"Useful to any librarian looking for protection or wondering where responsibilities end and liabilities begin. Recommended." (Academic Library Book Review)*

Archives and Library Administration: Divergent Traditions and Common Concerns, edited by Lawrence J. McCrank, PhD, MLS (Vol. 7, No. 2/3, 1986). *"A forward-looking view of archives and libraries. . . . Recommend[ed] to students, teachers, and practitioners alike of archival and library science. It is readable, thought-provoking, and provides a summary of the major areas of divergence and convergence." (Association of Canadian Map Libraries and Archives)*

Excellence in Library Management, edited by Charlotte Georgi, MLS, and Robert Bellanti, MLS, MBA (Vol. 6, No. 3, 1985). *"Most beneficial for library administrators . . . for anyone interested in either library/information science or management." (Special Libraries)*

Marketing and the Library, edited by Gary T. Ford (Vol. 4, No. 4, 1984). *Discover the latest methods for more effective information dissemination and learn to develop successful programs for specific target areas.*

Finance Planning for Libraries, edited by Murray S. Martin (Vol. 3, No. 3/4, 1983). *Stresses the need for libraries to weed out expenditures which do not contribute to their basic role–the collection and organization of information–when planning where and when to spend money.*

Collection Development
in the Electronic Environment:
Shifting Priorities

Sul H. Lee
Editor

Collection Development in the Electronic Environment: Shifting Priorities has been co-published simultaneously as *Journal of Library Administration,* Volume 28, Number 4 1999.

The Haworth Information Press
An Imprint of
The Haworth Press, Inc.
New York • London • Oxford

Published by

The Haworth Information Press, 10 Alice Street, Binghamton, NY 13904-1580 USA

The Haworth Information Press is an imprint of The Haworth Press, Inc., 10 Alice Street, Binghamton, NY 13904-1580 USA.

Collection Development in the Electronic Environment: Shifting Priorities has been co-published simultaneously as *Journal of Library Administration,* Volume 28, Number 4 1999.

Cover design by Thomas J. Mayshock Jr.

Library of Congress Cataloging-in-Publication Data

Collection development in the electronic environment : shifting priorities / Sul H. Lee, editor.
     p. cm.
     A series of papers presented at a conference hosted by the University of Oklahoma Libraries in cooperation with the University of Oklahoma Foundation on March 4 and 5, 1999.
     "Co-published simultaneously as Journal of library administration, volume 28, number 4 1999."
     Includes bibliographical references and index.
     ISBN 0-7890-0964-1 (alk. paper)–ISBN 0-7890-0982-X (alk. paper)
     1. Academic libraries–Collection development–United States–Congresses. 2. Libraries–United States–Special collections–Electronic information resources–Congresses. I. Lee, Sul H.
Z675.U5 C64235 1999
025.3'44–dc21
                                                       99-057822

INDEXING & ABSTRACTING

Contributions to this publication are selectively indexed or abstracted in print, electronic, online, or CD-ROM version(s) of the reference tools and information services listed below. This list is current as of the copyright date of this publication. See the end of this section for additional notes.

- *Academic Abstracts/CD-ROM*
- *Academic Search: data base of 2,000 selected academic serials, updated monthly*
- *AGRICOLA Database*
- *BUBL Information Service, an Internet-based Information Service for the UK higher education community <URL: http://bubl.ac.uk/>*
- *Cambridge Scientific Abstracts*
- *CNPIEC Reference Guide: Chinese National Directory of Foreign Periodicals*
- *Current Articles on Library Literature and Services (CALLS)*
- *Current Awareness Abstracts of Library & Information Management Literature, ASLIB (UK)*
- *Current Index to Journals in Education*
- *Educational Administration Abstracts (EAA)*
- *Higher Education Abstracts*
- *IBZ International Bibliography of Periodical Literature*
- *Index to Periodical Articles Related to Law*
- *Information Reports & Bibliographies*
- *Information Science Abstracts*
- *Informed Librarian, The*
- *INSPEC*
- *Journal of Academic Librarianship: Guide to Professional Literature, The*
- *Konyvtari Figyelo-Library Review*
- *Library & Information Science Abstracts (LISA)*

(continued)

- *Library and Information Science Annual (LISCA)*
- *Library Literature*
- *MasterFILE: updated database from EBSCO Publishing*
- *Newsletter of Library and Information Services*
- *OT BibSys*
- *(PAIS) Public Affairs Information Service) NYC www.pais.org*
- *PASCAL, c/o Institute de L'Information Scientifique et Technique*
- *Referativnyi Zhurnal (Abstracts Journal of the All-Russian Institute of Scientific and Technical Information)*
- *Trade & Industry Index*

Special Bibliographic Notes related to special journal issues (separates) and indexing/abstracting:

- indexing/abstracting services in this list will also cover material in any "separate" that is co-published simultaneously with Haworth's special thematic journal issue or DocuSerial. Indexing/abstracting usually covers material at the article/chapter level.
- monographic co-editions are intended for either non-subscribers or libraries which intend to purchase a second copy for their circulating collections.
- monographic co-editions are reported to all jobbers/wholesalers/approval plans. The source journal is listed as the "series" to assist the prevention of duplicate purchasing in the same manner utilized for books-in-series.
- to facilitate user/access services all indexing/abstracting services are encouraged to utilize the co-indexing entry note indicated at the bottom of the first page of each article/chapter/contribution.
- this is intended to assist a library user of any reference tool (whether print, electronic, online, or CD-ROM) to locate the monographic version if the library has purchased this version but not a subscription to the source journal.
- individual articles/chapters in any Haworth publication are also available through the Haworth Document Delivery Service (HDDS).

For Melissa

Collection Development in the Electronic Environment: Shifting Priorities

CONTENTS

ABOUT THE EDITOR

Sul H. Lee, Dean of the University Libraries, University of Oklahoma, is an internationally recognized leader and consultant in the library administration and management field. Dean Lee is a past member of the Board of Directors, Association of Research Libraries, the ARL Office of Management Services Advisory Committee, and the Council for the American Library Association. His works include *The Impact of Rising Costs of Serials and Monographs on Library Services and Programs*; *Library Material Costs and Access to Information*; *Budgets for Acquisitions: Strategies for Serials, Monographs, and Electronic Formats*; *Vendor Evaluation and Acquisition Budgets*; *The Role and Future of Special Collections in Research Libraries*; *Declining Acquisitions Budgets*; and *Access, Ownership, and Resource Sharing.* He is also Editor of the *Journal of Library Administration.*

Introduction

Sul H. Lee

On March 4 and 5, 1999, the University of Oklahoma Libraries in cooperation with the University of Oklahoma Foundation hosted a conference, "Collection Development in the Electronic Environment: Shifting Priorities." The conference brought together librarians and vendors from around the country to discuss important issues facing the library profession. I am very pleased to present the papers given at this conference.

Carla Stoffle, Dean of Libraries at the University of Arizona, presented the first paper co-written by her, Janet Fore and Barbara Allen. The paper sets the tone for the conference by discussing change in higher education and the need for libraries to be part of that change. Ms. Stoffle uses the University of Arizona Libraries as a case study of change in structure, functions and activities. Paul J. Kobulnicky, Director of Libraries at the University of Connecticut, presented a paper by Richard C. Fyffe and Paul J. Kobulnicky, which continued the discussion of change in information access and collection development. Mr. Kobulnicky argues that today's university environment challenges the traditional collection-centered model and research libraries must identify scholar needs and develop programs to meet those needs.

Fred Lynden, Associate Librarian, Technical Services, at Brown University, focuses his paper on collection budgeting issues. Mr. Lynden uses Brown University experiences to discuss budget processes and politics, user education and issues associated with electronic resources. Olivia Madison, Dean of Library Services at Iowa State University, describes in her paper how a serials cancellation project led to university-wide development of a new vision for the library.

Deborah Jakubs, Director, Collection Services at Duke University, examines staffing for collection development in an electronic environment. Again, our changing environment is leading to different models for collection

[Haworth co-indexing entry note]: "Introduction." Lee, Sul H. Co-published simultaneously in *Journal of Library Administration* (The Haworth Information Press, an imprint of The Haworth Press, Inc.) Vol. 28, No. 4, 1999, pp. 1-2; and: *Collection Development in the Electronic Environment: Shifting Priorities* (ed: Sul H. Lee) The Haworth Information Press, an imprint of The Haworth Press, Inc., 1999, pp. 1-2. Single or multiple copies of this article are available for a fee from The Haworth Document Delivery Service [1-800-342-9678, 9:00 a.m. - 5:00 p.m. (EST). E-mail address: getinfo@haworthpressinc.com].

development. Ms. Jakubs discusses some of these models in her paper. Barbara McFadden Allen, Director, Committee on Institutional Cooperation's Center for Library Initiatives and Assistant Director of the CIC, furthers the discussion on collection development by identifying some of the conditions influencing present-day libraries and then suggesting collaboration as a means of serving libraries.

The last two papers were presented by representatives from the vendor community, providing interesting insight into priorities and innovation. Karen Hunter, Senior Vice President, Elsivier Science, Inc., provides insight into setting priorities to meet the needs of their different customers. John J. Walsdorf, Vice President, Library Relations, for Blackwell's Book Services, completed the papers by reporting on his survey to book vendors in which he asked how they are using technology in their business.

As with past conferences, the papers stimulated fascinating discussion. It is my hope the presentation of these papers will continue to provoke thought and further discussion within the library profession. I want to thank all the contributors to this volume for their thoughtful papers. I also want to thank Mr. Don Hudson, who coordinated the conference from beginning to end, and Melanie Davidson and Wilbur Stolt for their work in producing this volume.

Developing New Models
for Collection Development

Carla J. Stoffle
Janet Fore
Barbara Allen

For the last month, I have been drafting the chapter examining the human, physical, fiscal, and academic resources for the University of Arizona's North Central Accreditation self-study. This is an interesting exercise anytime, but an especially useful one while working on this paper about collection development. One of the major challenges of any accreditation self-study is to demonstrate the institution's present success in utilizing its resources to achieve learning, research, and service goals. At the same time the study must identify how the institution uses its resources to meet the challenges of the future. It is especially difficult to provide the data to support the new directions when current institutional success is measured primarily in terms of inputs. However, future success will almost surely be measured in terms of outcomes. For example, how much have students learned and do they demonstrate that they are capable of continued learning?

At the institutional level, we do not yet have enough experiences in identifying the most important outcomes, creating ways to measure outcomes, making specific outcomes institutional priorities or holding units accountable for outcomes.

We are used to institutional environments characterized by, "Give us more and we will teach more." Or: "If you give us more we will improve student

Carla J. Stoffle is Dean of Libraries, University of Arizona.
Janet Fore is Undergraduate Services Librarian, University of Arizona Library.
Barbara Allen is Program Coordinator, University of Arizona Library.

[Haworth co-indexing entry note]: "Developing New Models for Collection Development." Stoffle, Carla J., Janet Fore, and Barbara Allen. Co-published simultaneously in *Journal of Library Administration* (The Haworth Information Press, an imprint of The Haworth Press, Inc.) Vol. 28, No. 4, 1999, pp. 3-15; and: *Collection Development in the Electronic Environment: Shifting Priorities* (ed: Sul H. Lee) The Haworth Information Press, an imprint of The Haworth Press, Inc., 1999, pp. 3-15. Single or multiple copies of this article are available for a fee from The Haworth Document Delivery Service [1-800-342-9678, 9:00 a.m. - 5:00 p.m. (EST). E-mail address: getinfo@haworthpressinc.com].

3

learning by introducing new technologies and techniques." We also ask for more to do research and to provide more programs for the community. To make the existing system continue to work at a high quality level requires significant amounts of old and new money.

We, of course, do need money for legitimate purposes such as maintaining competitive salaries (80% of our budget), upgrading networking and computing capability, innovative teaching, maintaining and modernizing aging physical facilities, and maintaining a traditionally acquisitions-oriented library while building the digital library for the future.

Yet, there is not a lot more money. State support is falling as a proportion of our revenues. In the 1970s, state legislature on the average allocated as much as 25% of their budget to higher education; today that percentage is down to close to 15% (Atwell, 1994). Taxpayers (or legislators in their name) want us to do more with less as business and industry have done over the most recent decade. They want to be sure that we have applied good business practices to the business of higher education and they want us to be more accountable. They do not want to know what our peer institutions get or spend unless it is less. They are not concerned with our rising costs and don't want to hear that it takes more to do the same.

We have to discover ways to talk to legislatures and other constituencies and to educate them on the incredible cost-effective services we can provide as well as the valuable role we play in the society. Having a focus on outcomes and outcomes-based criteria is the vital approach we must take while initiating these discussions. Therefore a focus on outcomes and outcome-based criteria is a vital institutional question.

We can begin these discussions at the institutional level by adopting a shared vision. This is necessary in order to replace the current models and build new ones. Yet it is difficult for a shared vision to emerge when we are talking about a transformation in how we do our major functions. A shared vision requires that we smash the beautiful and old container we carried our thinking in and move to use the many pieces to build a brand new vessel–one that is beautiful and functional, too, but looks nothing like the old container.

These institutional problems trickle down to the library where they are magnified by library problems, such as:

- Inflationary increases for paper and electronic collections yearly averaging in double digits,
- Needs for new technologies and their maintenance which yearly fall into the tens, if not hundreds, of thousands of dollars, and
- Need for staff with new skills that are different from skills needed in the past.

Does this sound familiar? I suspect so. The University of Arizona is not too different from every other major public research university, or maybe any public institution of higher education. But what do these problems have to do with our conference focus on collection development, shifting paradigms and new models? I would suggest to you everything.

Libraries exist in, and are products of, the institutional setting. We cannot escape the problems of our institutions. In fact, we often face these problems earlier than most other units or before the institution recognizes their pervasiveness. We are central resources and exist for the whole, not any one part. We are bell-weather units and our effectiveness and health reflects the health of the campus. I believe this is true today and I believe it will be true in the university of the 21st century, but I am wary at the same time.

Just as our institutions face substantial economic challenges, they have new competitors that will force the transformation of public universities or they will have to accept relegation to a marginal role. Libraries are in the same position, only more so. Libraries must begin to demonstrate added value to institutional outcome priorities and we do not have the luxury of waiting for the institution to agree on these outcomes. We have to anticipate change and take risks. We cannot merely manage these changes; we must lead and be helpful in the institutional transformation. If not it is likely we will be irrelevant to the university that emerges in the next century.

Therefore, we must transform our libraries. We must develop a revolutionary vision and take steps to implement it each day. Transformation will not just happen or be the result of unrelated, small changes over time. Changes at the margin do not lead to transformation. Changes have to be made in the core areas and in how we think about core functions, such as collection development.

In this environment, we must take action before we know all of the answers or see clearly how to achieve our goals. We must be learners and problem solvers; we must learn as we do and be prepared to change course when things don't work. We must continually assess the needs of our customers and use this data to form our decisions. We must identify and measure our performance based on customer outcomes and customer satisfaction. We must see technology as providing us with powerful new tools to solve our problems, rather than as the problem or the driver of the changes we have to make. We must commit ourselves to being activists–driving the development of the technologies and facilitating the creation of new scholarly communication processes and knowledge products. We must be at the front of the knowledge creation and teaching/learning process chains, working as partners with the faculty.

We must adopt new work, such as electronic publishing, knowledge management, and educational design and be prepared to be equal partners or fierce competitors with our vendors, suppliers, publishers, etc., as the situation demands. We must take seriously and grow our role as information advocates. We must work with faculty so they are aware of copyright and fair use implications. We must work with legislators, administrations and faculty so they understand and absorb how the information market works and the implications for academic freedom on arbitrary and monopolistic pricing of academic publications.

We must approach our work differently and, in fact, have to stop thinking about "our work." Instead we must focus on the work of our customers. We must develop an orientation to outcomes and create performance measures which measure outcomes. We must move away from adhering to current activities, programs, policies, roles, and services just because they were successful in the past. We must question everything. Everyone in the organization must develop leadership skills and take leadership roles for specific situations. All staff has to understand, and be empowered to act on, the library's vision in order to ensure they are doing the right things, rather than just doing things right. There is no formula or checklist. We must create new paradigms and employ people who can work in an environment of change and ambiguity. We must create new organizational structures to accomplish the above and all must be based on our shared vision, professional values, institutional mission or purpose, and customer needs.

While the above will be hard work, it is not impossible and it is very worthwhile doing. I know whereof I speak because The University of Arizona Library for nearly six years has been undergoing the kind of transformation described in the foregoing.

The impetus for our radical changes was the Task Force on Access and Ownership Study and Report. This report called for a rethinking of our collection development function and for moving our focus from artifacts and the management of artifacts to a focus on customers and their information needs (Brin and Cochran, 1994). Couched in terms of access, the recommendations urged the Library to look to the future and the potential of the new technology to help us move to an information management concept. It recommended our primary goal become meeting customer information needs in the shortest turnaround time possible. This "rethinking" was based on the economics of the print ownership and print information management environment. The continued growth in the cost of buying print was making it impossible to successfully meet the needs of the campus. Out of this report came the realization that we did not have the luxury of completely maintaining the traditional print-based library while we built the digital library.

There have been some interesting decisions and consequences resulting from our changes in our thinking about the collection development function and a focus on our customers. I would like to share some of these today in the spirit that there may be some insights and some approaches that would be useful to you. It is my hope that using a case approach to present some of the issues will provide a richer experience and will raise some questions that you can explore further either with myself or the other presenters. This is not intended to be a how we "done it good." Nor do I intend to imply that Arizona is the new model for academic libraries. Let me assure you, we don't have all the answers and aren't sure we are even asking the right questions.

Let me begin with a little background information. In 1991, the University of Arizona Library had a very traditional research library organizational structure. We had 16 departments and four assistant directors (Appendix 1). We were organized around formats or our work–reference, acquisitions, media, maps, etc. "Book budget" allocation decisions were made by the assistant directors and the librarian with advice from the Collection Development Committee. Four bibliographers in acquisitions then carried out the majority of the actual collection development work in consultation with reference librarians.

We accepted thousands of gift books each year and added anything in scope that we did not already own to the collection. We used up considerable resources in the traditional binding and repair work including the replacement of missing pages in books and journals. We replaced lost books if they were in print and spent staff time searching out-of-print catalogs to identify items we did not own.

Our interlibrary loan function was an adjunct activity of reference that was run on an 8 to 5 Monday through Friday schedule. Average delivery times were from five to six weeks. At least three-fourths of our staff were involved in processing activities. We had at least 10 service points scheduled to be open at varying hours. Our digital resources consisted of a few stand-alone CD-ROMs and online commercial services. Librarians did all online searches and spent most of their time in the library.

Today, our structure is quite different and is based on our values of continual learning, customer focus, diversity, integrity and flexibility. Now, we are organized into functional and cross-functional teams, not departments. We deliberately chose the team structure because we wanted to capture the creativity inherent in our staff and unleash front line staff to make decisions that enable customers to achieve their information goals. We wanted to delegate decision-making authority and have units able to respond more quickly to changes in customer needs in specific segments of the campus and to the rapidly changing information environment. We wanted to increase productivity and our problem-solving capability.

In our current organization chart (Appendix 2) we have eliminated the assistant director level and shifted those responsibilities to teams or standing cross-functional teams. We have organized our front line functional teams to reflect the organization of our customers in their academic departments/colleges. There are Social Science, Fine Arts Humanities, Science Engineering, and Research, Archives Museum Teams. And as a reflection of the University's growing commitment to undergraduates, the library has an Undergraduate Services Team. We call these teams integrative services (IS) teams and almost all librarians now work on these public-oriented teams. Integrative service librarians are responsible for needs assessment, education, information resource development, in-depth information provision, knowledge management, and connection development for their customer groups. It is the job of these librarians to integrate the library's services and information resources to meet customer needs and make customers as self-sufficient as possible.

The integrative services teams are supported by four functional teams: Technical Services, Materials Access, Library Information Support, and the Financial and Administrative Services. These teams focus on the internal functions of the library. They pay bills, maintain and improve technology, order and process materials, and make sure materials are accessible, electronically and physically. Ultimately, the goal of these teams is to organize so that integrative librarians can be outwardly focussed on our primary customers–faculty and students.

Integrative services librarians are very visible on campus. They have office hours in dorms, computer labs and academic departments. Many librarians are listed as co-instructor on class syllabi; faculty and librarians co-author scholarly articles.

For many librarians, the information resource role was new in 1993 and it was defined to encompass the following:

- Identify subject materials and information resources in all formats for purchase;
- Identify alternative sources for materials not owned–resource sharing possibilities, licenses, document delivery;
- Manage the budget for each subject area responsibility;
- Conduct needs assessment and evaluation studies and monitor curriculum and research issues and trends;
- Create and monitor performance measures (outcomes);
- Create approval plan profiles and monitor the performance of the plans;
- Monitor information policy issues that might impact customer groups and regularly communicate these, for example, copyright and intellectual property, filtering, and licensing issues;
- Develop gateways and access paths to information on the Internet; and
- Identify local collections that should be converted to an electronic format and made available over the network.

Librarians have the freedom to carry out these functions in a variety of ways and have received training for their new roles. In the near future, integrative service librarians will begin to use the new BNA Collection Manager product. Collection Manager provides the flexibility needed to support the fundamental elements of collection development–identification, evaluation, selection, and acquisition of materials. It also provides a tool to help librarians hold themselves accountable because it allows staff to manage their own budgets and to articulate the reasons a selection decision was made. This product will allow them to better monitor the effectiveness of their approval plans and to easily identify related publications not on the plan that are relevant. Ordering will be done online at selection time and materials will be received pre-processed.

This will reduce by weeks the time from selection to the shelves. This time reduction will certainly aid in selling the "just-in-time" collection philosophy to faculty who are still "just-in-case" oriented. It will also reduce library costs for ordering and processing so that those dollars can be reallocated to strategic priorities. Clearly, Collection Manager will change how we do collection management and we are able to be early adopters of such a product for several reasons. First, our partnership stance has opened us up to opportunities like this with BNA–we have worked together on product development. Second, our values and customer focus make us more open and flexible. We are willing to try things out even if they will lead to work changes and job elimination. Staff has the confidence that if their jobs change or are eliminated there will be place for them in the library. The library is committed to moving people on to learn new responsibilities; this is our preference and not laying people off.

An important organizational addition to the collection management function is the creation of the standing Information Resource Council (IRC). This cross-functional team makes allocation and policy decisions for information resources development, creation, management, and preservation. The majority of its members are representatives from the integrative service's teams. The members of IRC actually spend the information access budget based on customer needs.

The purpose of the Information Resource Council is to provide leadership, vision, and strategic direction for information resources development, creation, management, and preservation.

The charge of the Council is to:

- Articulate a library-wide vision of the desired information environment
- Allocate and manage the information access budget
- Identify, implement, and evaluate strategies to ensure and enhance current and ongoing customer access to information
- Communicate with and educate selectors and other customers about the current situation, policies, and directions of information resources

Their scope encompasses:

- Development of policies and resolution of macro level issues related to information resources development and creation
- Management and preservation for all formats in all units of the University of Arizona Library
- Stewardship and allocation of the information access budget
- Collaboration with teams to develop performance measures and criteria to measure selector effectiveness

The Council allocates the information access budget using guideline policies and assumptions agreed upon with Library Cabinet, the Library's leadership group. The Information Resource Council is expected to communicate regularly with integrative service librarians, indeed, with any library staff who has a stake in the information budget.

The Council is expected to produce a timely allocation of the information access budget as well as strategies that will guide the development, creation, preservation and management of information resources. Also Council members are expected to be leaders in educating selectors and our external customers. The goal is to have knowledgeable and informed constituents inside and outside the library so that they have access to information that promotes teaching, learning and research.

IRC works with the IS teams to establish performance measures for the total effort as well as for selector effectiveness. In the past few years, the IRC has undertaken to create a resource allocation mechanism based on customer data such as number of majors, credit hours taught, use of the collection, and publication and research revenue generation, and has conducted surveys to determine customer needs and satisfaction. IRC has developed selector training materials and programs, established a set of policies for selectors to work within and has taken the lead on developing packets for selectors to use for communicating policy issues to faculty.

It has also adopted licensing guidelines based on principles of access and fair use, established consortia for licensing and buying materials, created resource sharing agreements, and formalized a shared staffing for Slavic selection with Arizona State University. It has formulated policies that over the next few years will lead to the removal of print materials from the shelves when they are duplicated by the electronic access. IRC has increased funding for document delivery (nearly $250,000 annually), formulated a plan to replace most of the print reference collection with electronic resources, and supported and set aside dollars to begin our electronic publishing efforts. Next year, the University of Arizona Library will devote approximately 20% of its information access budget to access activities.

Reflecting this institution's activist stance, the IRC has approved the University of Arizona Library's founding membership of SPARC and is committed to cancelling high cost journals as the new SPARC-generated products are available. Finally, remember that they, not the dean, make these and other decisions having to do with book replacement, binding, and collection maintenance. The library has actually implemented shared decision making in the most critical budget area.

Two other units need some description. The first is Interlibrary Loan. Interlibrary Loan has moved from reference to the Information Access team, and now is part of the Materials Access team. All of these moves reflect a change in our perception of the role and goals of the unit. The shift to Information Access reflected the view that the unit was focussed on obtaining materials. The shift to Materials Access reflects the perspective that it is the delivery of the materials to the customer that is the focus. After undergoing a process improvement study, the unit reduced turnaround time, delivered articles directly to the customer via mail, fax, or e-mail, and reduced staff while doubling the number of requests. Interlibrary loan requests are dealt with seven days a week and go out within four hours. Materials are available all hours the Main Library circulation desk is open. Books are received mostly within 16 days and over half the articles requested arrived within six days.

This unit, by developing customer-focussed performance measures and by examining their processes, has built a remarkable ability to be flexible. This past year their vendor offering online document delivery eliminated the service; interlibrary loan was able to relocate a new vendor and services without missing a heartbeat. Our customers never knew there was a change in our supplier.

There is still much more to do here, but if "just-in-time" information management is to be a reality, access time has to drop to 24 or 48 hours. The staff of this unit now understand the priorities and are focussed on the work of our customers. They are constantly looking for ways to remove barriers and for ways to enhance direct customer self-sufficiency. They have switched from doing things right to doing the right things. They have established performance measures accordingly. They also conduct regular customer satisfaction surveys to identify outcomes and changes on which they should concentrate.

One other unit, the Digital Library Initiatives Group (DLIG), is illustrative of the University of Arizona approach to information management. DLIG is a recently created cross-functional team with three permanent staff and project staff, as needed, loaned from the functional teams. For its first three incipient years, DLIG is charged with developing a vision and plan for how the University of Arizona Library will move into knowledge management and electronic publishing. It will also engage in strategic projects that deliver needed information to support campus initiatives while they build the knowledge and skill of the staff.

The Digital Library Initiatives Group will initiate electronic publishing and text creation projects that move the library forward in enhancing access and preserving collections. The DLIG is providing the structure for staff to create new means of scholarly communication. Additionally they are developing technical expertise among all staff members as well as researching digital application and human interaction.

The DLIG's primary initiatives include:

- *Southwest E Text Center.* Working with subject area librarians, staff in the DLIG will scan appropriate materials related to the southwest. In the process, what is learned about copyright, metadata, Web-based selection of materials will be discussed, so that there is a shared understanding on what is involved in publishing new knowledge packages.
- *Images and Archives.* In an effort to support the university's curriculum and research needs, the DLIG will create new exhibits and expand existing exhibits related to the Southwest and our unique collections.
- *Electronic Journals and Reference Resources.* In this project the DLIG will work in collaboration with integrative service teams to develop a plan and priorities for the migration of selected reference sources and journals from print to electronic format. One of the goals here is to explore opportunities for alternative means of scholarly communications.
- *Electronic Reserves.* Over the course of the 1998/99 academic year the DLIG has worked to selectively digitize approximately 50% of the 11,000 articles currently in paper form in the Reserve Services area.

For further information see: www.library.arizona.edu/library/teams/access98/ aptdig4.htm

The job titles of staff working in the DLIG are indicative of the new work of the library. For instance on that team there is an Intellectual Property and Scholarly Communications Librarian. Her role is to consult with faculty regarding curriculum-related copyright issues, especially those relating to electronic format. She works directly with staff from the Library and other Faculty Development partnership units to provide support for faculty and curriculum development.

There is also a Data Services Librarian. This position plans and develops formalized data services programs, including access to geospatial and data sets that can be incorporated into the curriculum in order to enhance the academic experience.

The Meta Data Librarian establishes relationships with potential campus partners, takes a leadership role on campus related to academic metadata and plays an integral part in the implementation of the Library's digital initiatives.

DLIG is also focussed on the responsibility of the library to provide access and to manage all types of information; not just information considered library information. By this we mean data sets, campus data, video and audio data, etc. Through DLIG, the library will move to the front of the knowledge creation chain providing skills and support for faculty.

At this point, there are at least three more topics that need to be addressed to put the foregoing in context. First, as you have probably already observed, the University of Arizona Library has created new language for our activities. For example, some of you may be thoroughly annoyed by now by our use of the word customer. We consciously created new terms because we felt this was necessary so that people would not fall into old patterns and behaviors. It symbolically helps us break with the past. It forces us to continually focus on our revolutionary vision and to think differently about information, not books, and about information provision, not reference.

Second, it needs to be acknowledged here that the only new money the Library has received in the last five years is for maintaining the collections and staying open 24 hours. Everything–the new organization, DLIG, equipment support–has been accomplished through streamlining, process improvement, and reallocation. The University of Arizona Library has eliminated nearly 30 positions and reallocated another 10-15 to fund the future. In the process, no one has been laid off or lost their job because of the changes. Training and support have been provided to staff to prepare them for the new work, and the underlying personnel compensation systems have been adjusted to reinforce the new organizational values and commitments. Performance measures and a focus on outcomes while in their infancy are entrenched in the organizational culture, as is the commitment to shared decision making. Staff are empowered, and are developing the skills, to make decisions about how best to meet customer needs in the context of the mission and values of the organization.

And perhaps most importantly: our customers are reacting positively to what we have ben doing. The university administration is very supportive. Faculty and students like many of our improvements, such as reduced ordering and processing times, improved shelf availability for what we do own, processing improvements in interlibrary loan and reserves, etc. Faculty also like the help we are providing in redesigning their courses. But many faculty members are still print and ownership oriented. They are only beginning to appreciate digital access and this may be because many have only recently had access to appropriate equipment and training. Also, students are impatient that we haven't moved faster and that things don't work perfectly.

Believe it or not, I could go on and on, but let me stop here. I do want to stress that I have used the University of Arizona Library as an example and I do not expect you to be able to take what we have done and impose it on your library. What I would like for each of you to do is to make a decision that you can create the future. Use what you have learned here to develop your own revolutionary vision and identify what the first step might be to realize it. Remember, if it is not possible in your mind, it is not possible!

REFERENCES

Atwell, Robert H. *Higher Education and the Path to Progress, New Directions for Higher Education. Number 85*, Spring, 1994, p. 127.
Brin, Beth and Elissa Cochran. *Access and Ownership in the Academic Environment: One Library's Progress Report. The Journal of Academic Librarianship*, 20:4, September 1994, p. 207-212.

APPENDIX 1. Organizational Chart, University of Arizona Library, 1991

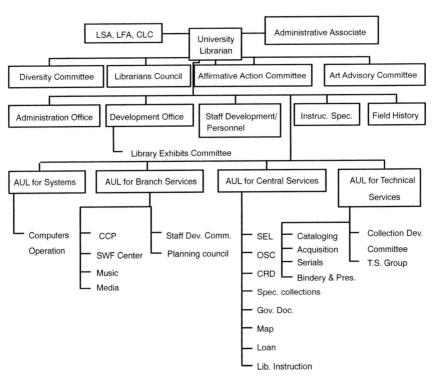

APPENDIX 2. University of Arizona Library Organization Chart 3/99

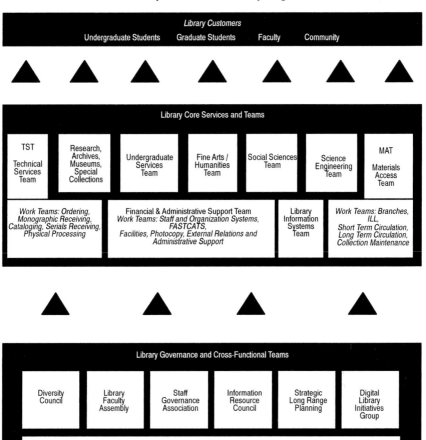

Negotiating the Soul of the Library: Change Management in Information Access and Local Collection Development

Richard C. Fyffe
Paul J. Kobulnicky

INTRODUCTION: INFORMATION ACCESS PARADIGMS IN HIGHER EDUCATION HAVE SHIFTED

As we seek answers to society's complex problems, many of us look back with some affection to what we believed were simpler times. Rightly or wrongly, we think that yesterday's regional and national economics were easier to understand than are today's global economics. We think that the pace of a world built on simple machines was more humane than the pace of one built with transistors, not to mention integrated circuits. Not only has our world gotten more complex, but the rate at which that complexity grows seems to have increased. In this dramatically changing environment, there is a striking difference between the historical stability of institutions of higher education and the rapid evolution of the societies of which those institutions are a part.

Richard C. Fyffe is Area Head, Collections Services, Homer Babbidge Library, University of Connecticut.

Paul J. Kobulnicky is Vice Chancellor for Information Services, Homer Babbidge Library, University of Connecticut.

Author note: The term "soul" is derived from Leon Litwack's "Has the library lost its soul?" *California Monthly* 108 (Feb. 1998). http://www.alumni.berkley.edu/monthly/monthly_index/feb_98/library.html (10 March 1999).

[Haworth co-indexing entry note]: "Negotiating the Soul of the Library: Change Management in Information Access and Local Collection Development." Fyffe, Richard C., and Paul J. Kobulnicky. Co-published simultaneously in *Journal of Library Administration* (The Haworth Information Press, an imprint of The Haworth Press, Inc.) Vol. 28, No. 4, 1999, pp. 17-35; and: *Collection Development in the Electronic Environment: Shifting Priorities* (ed: Sul H. Lee) The Haworth Information Press, an imprint of The Haworth Press, Inc., 1999, pp. 17-35. Single or multiple copies of this article are available for a fee from The Haworth Document Delivery Service [1-800-342-9678, 9:00 a.m. - 5:00 p.m. (EST). E-mail address: getinfo@haworthpressinc.com].

17

That cultural gulf has caused many people to wonder if higher education is properly responsive to the contemporary needs of the community.

During the period between the Second World War and the middle 1980s, higher education experienced dramatic growth. A booming economy fueled by expanding foreign markets demanded an increasingly skilled workforce whose training was provided by colleges and universities. Technological innovation was accelerating, moreover, in part because of the research conducted at those universities. Through increased tuition revenues, state and federal support for instruction, and federal funding for research, universities expanded as in no other time in our history. However, the period of boom began to decline in the late 1980s, and by the 1990s growth in higher education had braked nearly to a halt.

As it approaches the year 2000, higher education is struggling to demonstrate its importance to a disenchanted community. Increases in the costs of higher education continue to outstrip similar costs in other sectors of the economy. To match those increases, higher education is faced either with increasing tuition or, in the case of public institutions, with receiving increased support from government sectors. Consumers, however, do not see the value of higher education increasing in the same proportion as tuition. Governments, in turn, trying desperately to reduce spending in all sectors, see little public support for increased subvention of higher education. At the same time, direct government sponsorship for university research is also declining, especially in the pure sciences, social sciences, and humanities.

As the world economy has moved from agriculture through industrialization, from local to global, the direct connection between research at the university and economic gain by the community has been seriously weakened. As a result, society is increasingly questioning the value of the research university. With declining or stable resources and increasing costs, growth across the university is difficult to sustain.[1]

Research universities are therefore forced to consider investing their limited resources selectively, to strengthen the operations that are likely to have greatest value over time. Not every worthwhile activity can be funded. Highly skilled faculty and staff demand competitive salaries, and salaries for faculty and staff can account for more than 75% of university budgets. Technology investments are required in all aspects of the institution, not simply in the sciences or in libraries. Consumer-oriented students are demanding "anytime, anyplace" programs as well as sophisticated physical and programmatic amenities on their campuses. To provide programs that attract a more diverse student population, the breadth of course offerings continues to increase. Thus, at a time when the library, "the heart of the university,"[2] demands increasing resources to maintain its relative position based on traditional models of successful practice, it is now being viewed as just one of many worthy applicants for its institution's budgetary attention.

During the post-war period of growth in higher education, university research libraries, too, experienced rapid growth. Information was relatively inexpensive, money was plentiful and, especially in the immediate post-war period, bulk collections from poor or war-ravaged nations were available for the asking.[3] Research libraries grew by acquisition, and a key measure of success for a research library, as it had been through the previous 2000 years, was the size of its collections. There was, at that time, compelling justification for this focus on size. Bigger was better because personal mobility and primitive telecommunications placed limits on scholarly work, and therefore the immediate availability of local holdings made a critical contribution to research productivity. It is worth noting that it was during the late 1950s through the 1970s that our current senior faculty acquired their information access habits.

In today's university environment, however, the collection-centered model for a research library must be broadened to include other models of successful library service. Not only do libraries face stiff competition for funds with other campus agencies, but the inflationary economics of scholarly publishing are fast undermining our ability to succeed within that model. At the same time, some of the scholarly functions previously performed only by local collections can now be performed by other kinds of information services. The challenge facing research libraries today is to identify the essential scholarly functions and then to develop information programs that fulfill those functions by using a variety of services–all the while seeking budgetary flexibility and efficiency.

Over the past 15 years, annual inflation in publishing has far outstripped increases in institutional budgets.[4] Universities have been forced to question the value of spending significantly more money to acquire the same amount of information, or of spending even more money to keep pace with increasing output. Chief academic offices were willing, early in the inflation cycle, to treat inflation rates as a short-term fluctuation and to support such investments; but inflation has persisted and competing forces for institutional resources have become too strong to ignore.

Brian Hawkins presents a dramatic illustration of the combined effects of inflation and increasing publishing rates on the collections model of the modern university research library. Hawkins posits a hypothetical library that in 1980 could acquire all of the world's published information. Factoring together inflation in material costs, growth rates in publishing, and average rates of increase in research library budgets, he concludes that "available budgets in 2001 will only be able to purchase 2% of what they had twenty years before" and further that "collections will be archiving something of the order of one-tenth of 1% of the available information."[5]

Inflation and publishing rates were not the only external factors affecting research libraries during the 1980s and 1990s. Growth in the technology and information service markets has also created new budgetary pressures. Modern integrated library management software has helped to automate and transform standard library processes, but at significant additional cost. Modern telecommunications has required installation of thousands more network connections than had previously been needed. The computerization of publishing has spurred the development of digital information products that added functionality to print but has also added new costs to libraries for the same content. Attached to these new networks and necessary for accessing digital information are the hundreds of advanced computer workstations for both staff and patrons that libraries must now acquire and upgrade.

Students, faculty, and administrators alike expect modern access and delivery technologies to be available in every research library. Students expect all library resources to be available virtually. Students' perception of institutional quality, moreover, may be shaped by the institution's readiness to deliver library and other instructional services directly to their living space.[6] Scholars, too, expect to be able to use digital information resources whenever those are available. Many scholars, however, are at the same time reluctant to give up more traditional print-based formats for the same information. Libraries must therefore often purchase the same information twice, once in paper and again (usually for an added percentage of the paper cost) in digital formats. Moreover, implementing new technologies and services requires a commitment to local innovation and experimentation, and thus incurs additional costs in fiscal and human resources. All of these factors, together with many less significant ones, reduce the total institutional funds available for the purchase of collections and other information formats.

The broad societal forces currently affecting higher education and the dramatic changes in the information, computing, and telecommunications industries are unlikely to abate in the near future. Research universities and their libraries must therefore seek both greater flexibility in their budgetary commitments and a clear understanding, shared among all stakeholders, of the purposes served by local collections and other information services and the priorities among those purposes. Our traditional understanding of the contributions of local collections to research, learning, and the preservation of intellectual heritage, largely developed before the advent of modern telecommunications and digital storage, may require revision.

THE CHANGING OF CULTURAL NORMS
REQUIRES SHARED RISK

As the primary producers of the scholarly content that research libraries collect and make accessible–and therefore as direct contributors to the acceleration of publishing rates that threatens libraries' ability to meet their collecting aspirations–research faculty must share responsibility for institutional decisions about the future of local collections. Moreover, as consumers of that content, the faculty also have a direct stake in shaping that future. However, university faculty often have insufficient knowledge of either the economic realities of higher education and scholarly publication or the complex choices presented to libraries in the current information market. Without that kind of understanding, the challenges facing universities and libraries can too easily be regarded as a straightforward problem of insufficient funding. Learning about budgets and the new methods of information access is an investment of time and energy that busy researchers must weigh against the time lost for research itself. In addition, faculty have seldom been given real authority to make decisions about resources, and therefore have seen no real benefit to being informed.

Librarians bear some responsibility as well for faculty's lack of understanding of these issues. Local discussions of the current state of scholarly publishing have all too often been precipitated by the latest crisis in the serials budget, rather than being part of an examination of systemic change in scholarly communications. In order to move a research university to a new philosophical understanding of the roles of local collections in the context of information access, a dialectical process of mutual education must be undertaken.

If the faculty are not part of such a process, then the problem does indeed become "the library problem."[7] This was demonstrated most acutely in 1998 when a lack of faculty confidence caused the library director at the University of California at Berkeley to step down over what appeared to be the director's inability to garner a sufficient share of Berkeley's fiscal resources for the library. Leon Litwack, Pulitzer Prize-winning Professor of history and former chair of the University of California/Berkeley Senate Library Committee put it this way:

> The gravity of the crisis cannot be overstated. Without sustaining our print collections, Berkeley is simply not in the top tier of research and teaching universities. We may have an impressive, even a beautiful physical structure; but with diminished library resources and library staff and the difficulties in browsing, it is a library without a soul. If the library is, as many acknowledge, the heart of the University teaching

and research program, it has suffered a major stroke that threatens to incapacitate it in meeting the minimal needs of faculty and students.[8]

Given the prevailing increase in publishing rates, inflation in the costs of scholarly publications, and the new costs that must be borne by research libraries, the traditional model of extensive, self-sufficient, stand-alone local collections cannot be sustained. However, most of the measures associated with research libraries are still based on this old model. The annual membership index of the Association of Research Libraries is seen by many scholars (and librarians as well) as an ordered list of successful research libraries, despite the fact that its chief indicators are inputs (volumes added, dollars spent) rather than service measures.[9] There is little agreement among librarians–much less in the broader scholarly community–regarding alternative definitions of quality. However, if the primary metric that determines success is one based on collection size, then it is only to be expected that faculty frustration with serial cancellations and deferred acquisitions will continue.

If librarians are eventually to propose and implement new models of information delivery and new measures of successful service, then they must have the faculty's trust. However, the access library model to which many libraries are turning–one that combines local collections with remote-access electronic resources and commercial document delivery services–removes control over service standards from the local library. By its nature, the access model gives more control to third-party information providers, especially to commercial vendors who are responding in their products and pricing to market conditions. One highly visible and distressing illustration of this loss of control was the 1998 replacement of *Lexis/Nexis* with *Academic Universe*, in which significant amounts of information content were no longer available to academic library users who had come to rely on the older version. The access model is less stable and less predictable than its predecessor, and this volatility will cause many faculty to question its viability.

Earning the trust of the faculty is vital because the faculty largely determine the culture of a university, and their opinion determines the success or failure of an academic support unit such as the library. Faculty members are responsible for setting the university's research agenda and thus the focus for research collections. Faculty likewise determine the curricula of the courses offered and (in some disciplines more than in others) the research topics of students. Thus, to a large extent the faculty determine the information needed to support learning. Moreover, their longevity in the institution (unlike that of students) means that their perceptions of quality will endure over long periods of time. Finally, since faculty salaries represent the single largest annual expenditure in the institution, faculty opinion will command the attention of administrations concerned to ensure the best return on institutional investment.

In 1991, Richard Doherty, writing on the results of a set of focus group activities, described a series of "preferred futures" for libraries. The focus groups consisted primarily of provosts and library directors at forty-one research institutions. Doherty noted that while "faculty opinion has traditionally been a key element in *orchestrating* [our emphasis] successful change in higher education," "efforts by librarians to de-emphasize ownership are interpreted [by the faculty] as a failure to understand both the political environment and legitimate differences in research methodologies among disciplines."[10] If an organization such as the library is to make changes in its philosophical assumptions in preparation for the future, then faculty and librarians must share an understanding of that future.

In order to create shared visions, two elements are essential: information and power. No one can imagine a future without knowledge of the environment in which it will unfold and of the significant forces that are affecting it. However, if the faculty are to reach the point where they are willing to invest time and energy in becoming informed, they must also have a sense that they have power to shape that future. The library must be willing to work with faculty to build a truly shared vision instead of telling them what the future is and then asking for an endorsement. The library may lose some control in this process, but it can thereby gain a sense that the inevitable risks in this new and difficult marketplace are shared more widely.

THE UCONN PROCESS–CREATE A PHILOSOPHY AND INTERPRET IT FOR EACH PROGRAM

One of the keys to success in a shared visioning process is to work with a representative group for the sake of efficiency, and then to broaden the discussion. Individual faculty members cannot and will not speak for "the Faculty." Instead, a broad philosophy must be established and then used as a vehicle for further discussions in academic departments, centers, and institutes.

The University of Connecticut library staff recognized that in order to restructure the use of acquisitions budgets while maintaining positive and deep relationships with academic programs, the faculty would have to be engaged in a shared planning process. The outcome of such a process would be a new information access philosophy that could be interpreted and applied differentially to each academic program. Every institution must determine the process of education and planning within the constraints and opportunities of its own organization and culture. What follows in this section is a brief description of the University of Connecticut's experience.

The process began with an agreement among the Director of Libraries, the Libraries' Head of Collections Services, and the chair of the faculty library advisory committee that the future of local collection development should be a topic for committee discussion during the coming academic year. The Libraries had just concluded a significant serials cancellation, and therefore the topic had some urgency. The Libraries provided leadership by developing the process and by analyzing and framing the questions. The issues were consolidated into a series of four thematic discussions, each of which took place at one or two two-hour meetings over the course of an academic year. Summaries were created and disseminated immediately following each discussion, and the accuracy of each summary was confirmed before or during the subsequent meeting.

Over the following summer break, the Libraries' Head of Collections Services developed a first draft of a framework statement, and during the next academic year iterative drafts were extensively debated and refined until a statement was endorsed by the whole committee for public dissemination. In a parallel process, these drafts were reviewed with the library staff, especially the subject-oriented liaison librarians. Their comments and concerns were incorporated in versions that were returned to the faculty committee. Each draft elicited new areas of conflict or disagreement, both among the committee members and between faculty and librarians. As the next sections will suggest, it has not always been possible to resolve the disagreements. Positive movement toward a new position requires that conflicts be identified and articulated. However, it is crucial that conflict remain creative and not be allowed to undermine the process.

The interdepartmental composition of the faculty committee was a critical element in this process. This structure enabled faculty members with different disciplinary perspectives to speak to each other directly about their needs for collections and information access. Direct conversation of this kind, facilitated by librarians, is a more effective mechanism for creating shared understanding than is the "shuttle diplomacy" too often practiced by librarians as they take their issues from department to department. Another important element in the composition of the committee was the participation of the Dean of Students and a representative from the Graduate Student Senate. Thus the perspective of students was not lost in a process heavily dominated by faculty.

Once the framework statement has been presented to the academic administration, the document will be disseminated widely to the university community. At the same time, the Libraries' liaisons for each academic program will meet with students and faculty in each department to present the framework, engage in a similar process of dialectical education, and interpret the framework's implications for that discipline. A key tenet of our information access policy is that different disciplines will give different priorities to local collections, remote-access electronic resources, and document delivery services. It is only when this last discipline-specific step has been completed that the vision or philosophy can be considered to have been accepted.

COMPLEX ISSUES MUST BE ANALYZED BY INVESTIGATING DRIVING FORCES

The process of creating an explicit framework for the future development of research library collections must recognize the several distinct roles in the information access system, as well as the factors that motivate and affect each. The process must therefore address the interrelated system of information access and local collections, the opportunities and constraints of technology, and the impact of the information marketplace on libraries in addition to considering the current needs of faculty and students. The agents in this complex system include scholars and teachers, students, publishers, information vendors/distributors, libraries and librarians, university administrators, owners of intellectual property, telecommunications vendors, and even the general citizenry, which in one way or another pays to support higher education. The interests of these agents interact and dynamically affect one another. There are, therefore, few simple cause-effect relationships. Each action by one player affects the environment for the others.

In this environment, agents must learn to look beyond their immediate interests and achieve a broader understanding of their long-term good. The best result is not necessarily the one that maximizes the benefit of any single player but rather the one that maintains the most stable and predictable information environment and sustains the viability of all players. However, discovering where each player's long-term interest lies in the new models of collecting and access requires careful thought and analysis. In a complex system, successful past practices are not necessarily the best guides to sustainable future practice. Librarians and faculty must be willing to generate and review data, to move beyond anecdotal evaluation, and to assess options in terms of their consequences in a complex marketplace. Moreover, they need to separate the symbolic value of information and information formats from the measurable contribution of information services to the academic enterprise. Most important, librarians and faculty must be willing to acknowledge that information access is just one of many worthwhile investments that can be made by institutions of higher education with a limited pool of funds.

To launch this process of managing change in the future of collections and access, we asked our library advisory committee to discuss with us the following broad issues:

- How the academy is changing;
- What is valued in a research library and how success is measured;

- How we might define a core local collection; and
- How we should respond to the politics and the economics of the information marketplace.

While the purpose of the present paper is to describe the process and the
issues, the current form of our framework statement may be of interest to
readers, and can be found at the Libraries' Web site.[11] The following sections
describe the broad context within which the authors engaged the committee
members during the discussions. They do not necessarily represent conclusions reached by all the participants.

THE ACADEMY: CHANGING MORE SLOWLY THAN EXPECTED

In order to develop a plan for information access and local collections that
will be effective in the future, libraries have to understand the degree to
which the home institution is changing in such core activities as teaching,
research, and outreach. As we have suggested, the faculty is the group within
the university most in control of the institution's core practices. Therefore,
the degree to which they believe that fundamental change is occurring represents the degree to which they will consider change in the institution's support services to be necessary and deserving of support. The faculty should be
asked to gauge the degree to which their own practices of teaching and
learning, research, and service are changing, and how information delivery
should change accordingly.

There are several significant aspects in which the academy is changing,
and exploration of all of these is a useful starting point for discussions of the
future of information services. Changes in teaching and learning have probably generated the greatest attention during the late 1990s. There is extensive
debate within the academy, for instance, on students as customers of higher
education and on students as higher education's product.[12] To what degree is
the consumer behavior of students affecting the practice of the faculty, and
how should that behavior affect student and faculty demands on the library?
To what extent do the faculty believe information literacy and competence in
the use of information technology to be a desirable goal for their students'
education, and what kind of contribution ought the library to make to that
education? For institutions with graduate programs, what is the relationship
between graduate and undergraduate education from the faculty perspective,
and how does that relationship affect the definition of essential library services? To what degree is distance learning implemented in the institution and
how should the library's resources be apportioned to support distance learning initiatives? In general, to what extent are new learning models being

integrated into the university's instructional program, and what faculty expectations for collections and access follow from those models?

Teaching and learning are not the only areas in which the academy is changing. Scholarly practice, even in the arts and humanities, has become more collaborative, and collaboration increasingly spans institutional, regional, and national boundaries. Modern telecommunications enhance such collaborations and may enhance information access to support distributed scholarship. To what extent does collaborative scholarship affect the role of local collections in a library's provision of information access? Research and scholarship are also spanning disciplinary boundaries with increasing ease. Does interdisciplinary work challenge the ability of local collections to supply needed information? Research funding is increasingly directed toward the support of economic and social development as well as technology transfer, and faculty research areas consequently shift rapidly as funders shift their priorities. To what degree do the faculty recognize the impact of rapidly changing research concentrations on the provision of library services?

Not all subject disciplines will experience such changes in teaching, learning, and research to the same degree and at the same rate. Administrative leadership from presidents, provosts, deans, and department heads is one important catalyst of change and will differ in degree and emphasis from institution to institution. Moreover, in an increasingly competitive higher education environment, the programs of peer institutions can likewise motivate change. Over the past decade, the relationship of the professional schools to their practitioners has oriented many of those schools to more entrepreneurial practices, often causing economic and cultural conflict within the broader institution. To what extent do the faculty recognize these various factors within their university, their school, and their department, and are they prepared to speculate on how such forces should affect library collections and information access?[13] For all the debate about transformation within higher education, however, it is important to note that local faculties may not be experiencing change in their own teaching to the same degree that administrations are urging it or that the media are reporting it.

DEFINING SUCCESS:
THE ACCESS MODEL
IS NEITHER SIMPLE NOR UNIFORM ACROSS DISCIPLINES

The access model can be roughly characterized as one which emphasizes information delivery when the user needs it over the modality (local collections, remote access to electronic files, document delivery) through which the information is supplied. However, implementation of the access model must be analyzed in terms of rapidly shifting access and collecting economies and the dramatic differences in the effectiveness of access and collecting from discipline to discipline. Moreover, because research-level collecting continues to be a crucial form of access, the access model cannot be defined in terms of a simple contrast with the older collections-based model.

The access model is further complicated by two conflicting forces. On the one hand, advances in networked access to electronic information blur the line between ownership and access. If immediate availability is one of the primary values of locally owned collections–as distinguished from traditional interlibrary borrowing or commercial document supply–then in that respect networked access to full text and images may be superior to print collections which may be lost, damaged, or circulated to other users. On the other hand, assuring the long-term availability of information–another hallmark of print collections–remains a significant economic, legal, and technical challenge for the access model. It is unclear what kinds of economic and institutional mechanisms will be needed to assure the widespread availability of print information from a smaller number of repositories, or the migration of electronic information from platform to platform over successive generations of scholars and students. This is a particular concern in disciplines some of whose literature may fall into temporary neglect and which may therefore not generate the use that (in a market-based model) might assure preservation. Workers in those disciplines will want to be sure that forgotten or neglected literature will still be accessible for rediscovery or revivification. In that respect, the durability of local collections of print, microform, and other "hard copy" formats has demonstrated a valuable utility, despite our legitimate concerns about acidic paper and other fragile media.

Even if we believe that retrospective digitization may allow us to have our cake and eat it, too–that is, to combine the broad access of electronic distribution with the durability of print formats–we must recognize significant legal and economic challenges. Intellectual property owners control the distribution rights for precisely the material most likely to be requested in digital forms, and the financial resources required to digitize existing collections can only be deployed at the cost of some other opportunity. Furthermore, increased reliance on third-party information vendors decreases local control over the content and the presentation of that information. Information users, including the faculty, may find the volatility of this market disturbing. All of these considerations may cause the access model of information delivery to be questioned.

Ready adoption of the access model will also vary greatly by discipline, and some gross generalizations can be made with respect to a given discipline's willingness to accept and even favor an access model. Those disciplines that seek great currency of information are more likely to value access over ownership. Disciplines that are more interdisciplinary in nature may likewise be more willing to recognize the inability of a local collection to supply all needed resources and thus to accept access over ownership. Disciplines that have good abstracting and indexing resources and that can therefore obtain reliable citations will have more confidence in reliable delivery from access methods. Such generalizations have limited utility, however. As the access library model is developed and promoted, it is critical that specific disciplinary needs be understood and accommodated. One model will not fit all needs. Any new collections and information policy should recognize the need to consult with various academic programs and to construct plans that meet the differing needs of the various disciplines. Acceptance will more likely follow when the several faculties can see that the library understands these differences and is working creatively within its resources to customize the access model in support of programmatic excellence.

There are no simple answers to these challenges. Economic constraints and the needs of our users for broader forms of access necessitate a new approach to collections and information services. However, in formulating a new collections and access philosophy it is vital that members of the university community grasp the strengths, weaknesses, and complexities of the various forms of information access. Faculty should be asked to consider the degree to which they are already utilizing the access library through interlibrary loan and document delivery as opposed to traveling to multiple sites to complete their information gathering activities. They should be asked to comment on the degree to which their increased bibliographic awareness has increased their desire for information not held in local collections. They should be asked to discuss their need for rapid access to information and the degree to which they take advantage of technological integration between their information access activities and their scholarly production. Their answers to these questions will provide guidance on their use and acceptance of the access library model. The ultimate measure for success for research libraries is the success of the current and future academic enterprise. Faculty should be asked to identify those aspects of library information services that contribute to their research productivity and teaching accomplishments.

THE CORE COLLECTION:
STRONG COLLECTIONS TEND TO CORRELATE
WITH STRONG AND STABLE ACADEMIC PROGRAMS

Local research collections of some magnitude are necessary to support degree-granting programs at every level of the university. However, the core collection is an abstract concept that defies simple, collective agreement. Universities have traditionally had implicit contracts with their faculty and students to provide information resources sufficient to support instruction and research. As the library formulates its collection plans, it is relatively easy to identify resources necessary to support the more limited and clearly defined undergraduate curriculum. It is likewise relatively easy to build collections that support course-oriented first professional degrees. However, as the library considers the resources required for scholarly advanced degrees, especially the Ph.D., the distinction between support for instruction and support for research scholarship begins to blur.

Indeed, the very distinction between teaching and research will be questioned by some faculty. From the faculty standpoint, excellent classroom teaching is often stimulated by an active research program, and from the student's standpoint learning is significantly enhanced through engagement with the problems and processes of research. From the library's standpoint, however, the instruction/research distinction has greater salience. Support for course work requires that large numbers of students be served within relatively rigid timeframes. Moreover, many of the students in a given course are likely to draw on the same relatively small number of titles, and each time the course is offered some of the same titles will be needed. The economics of continuing multiple uses therefore tend to favor print ownership (and sometimes networked access), while document delivery will provide these students with poor service at higher institutional cost. Research projects, by contrast, tend to draw on a wider range of resources, and those resources tend to be more specialized and to have fewer users. Under these circumstances, access models (networked full text or document delivery) may be preferable.

The different perspectives of faculty and librarians tend to create conflict over the prospective scope and depth of local collections in an access model. A related area in which conflict may arise concerns the library's response to changes in faculty research interests. Local collections of research quality generally result from a sustained collecting effort conducted over many years, and great research library collections are most often the result of a long-term library effort to support continuing excellence in a coherent disciplinary research effort. Academic departments and individual researchers, however, are likely to shift their research projects many times over the same period. While library collecting–even at the research level–is generally broader than the work of a given scholar at a given time, the volatility of faculty interests nevertheless challenges the ability of libraries to develop deep collections that meet their needs. The challenge is intensified by the accelerating productivity of the global scholarly community; by the increasing speciation and recombination of academic disciplines; and by the focus of external funding agencies on research that meets immediate–but changing–social needs.

Candidates for faculty positions are seldom selected for the fit between their research interests and the strengths of library collections or the impact of their research agenda on library information services. Yet if universities and their faculty are to create truly effective local collections to support the activities of their carefully chosen members, or if universities see library resources as a critical element of institutional scholarly success, then the entire faculty must begin to understand the economic basis for correlating individual faculty research with local library collections and access models.

THE POLITICAL ECONOMY OF INFORMATION: RESEARCH INSTITUTIONS MUST ACT AS DEMANDING CONSUMERS

By itself, the access model will not solve the economic crises that have beset libraries for the last two decades. A simple shift from print to digital formats will not yield the economic relief needed to accommodate other institutional needs, and we cannot expect the commercial document delivery market to remain stable as libraries cancel more and more serial subscriptions. Rather, the degree to which research institutions successfully control their information future is directly related to the willingness of faculty and libraries to use their economic power to influence the information market to their long-term advantage. Typically, however, faculty are reluctant to acknowledge the market nature of scholarly publishing, and structural changes in information delivery will be impossible to achieve unless that reluctance is overcome.

We have already noted the dire effects of prevailing inflation rates in scholarly journals. Declines in universities' subvention of their scholarly presses have exacerbated the pressures placed by rising serial costs on scholarly monographs. Profit-sector scholarly publishers have been more interested in maximizing short-term profits and in exerting strong control over intellectual property than in preserving the scholarly communications system. Finally, the merger trend among scholarly publishers has created massive conglomerates like Reed-Elsevier and the Thompson Corporation that dominate market segments and seek to control broader information economies.[14]

The information marketplace takes advantage of a venerable academic culture–one that, given the pressures on today's academy, is focused more on success for today than on strategic movement to a sustainable future. Research faculty are under significant pressure from their departments and universities to secure grants and to publish in the most prestigious venues. Students tend to view the university from the limited-term perspective of their degree work. Libraries need to demonstrate to their administrations excellence in current services. Publishers seek to maximize their financial reserves until a new publishing model is ready for investment. As each agent in this system seeks to maximize its own short-term advantage, however, it squanders its power to create a better future.

Every dollar that is spent on library collections and information services

has an effect on the marketplace of publishing. Libraries can use their information budgets to influence market trends by focusing their expenditures on
progressive models and by limiting their expenditures with the most destructive publishers.[15] To do so, however, they require authorization and support
from the faculty. Working together, faculty and libraries need to be willing to
assess the real value of information products against their costs, and to refuse
to pay exorbitant fees for services whose use-value cannot be convincingly
demonstrated. Similarly, they need to recognize when a license or contract
unacceptably hinders the academic mission, and to be willing to do without
the product. By the same token, faculty and libraries should aggressively
support the purchase of products that deliver exceptional value.

The scholarly community itself wields the greatest power for transforming
the scholarly communications system. Collectively, scholars are both the
producers and the primary consumers of the scholarly literature. Every decision by a scholar to submit, review, or accept a paper for publication helps to
sustain or to transform the current situation. Faculty must come to understand
and to take responsibility for the consequences of choosing a journal in which
to publish or lending their reputation to an editorial board. Scholarly authors
should be urged to negotiate qualified grants of copyright to the publishers
with which they work, and to reserve the right–at the least–for free dissemination of their articles within their institution for teaching purposes.

In the final analysis, the crisis in scholarly publishing is not a library problem
and can be resolved only through the actions of scholars and academic administrators. Through a forward-looking framework for developing collections and
information services, however, libraries can help to lead the rest of the university
toward an understanding of the economics of scholarly information and a willingness to invest collections budgets strategically and responsibly.

CONCLUSION:
FACULTIES ARE LEARNING ABOUT INFORMATION ACCESS

At this writing, the University of Connecticut Libraries are midway
through a process of engaging faculty in the definition of information access
and the role of local collections at our institution. Our experience thus far
suggests that while the process will be lengthy the prospects for success are
good. Scholarly societies and national media have already raised general
faculty awareness of the economic issues involved in scholarly communication. The process we have outlined is now helping to sharpen that general
awareness and to demonstrate the choices that we face within our own institution.

Several factors are critical in the development and implementation of a
process of this kind. Librarians need to recognize that the faculty still control

the culture in higher education and that the research library, as Litwack so eloquently describes, is a cultural icon of the institution. If change in research library collections is to be effectively managed, then the faculty must be engaged in the process of redefining expectations for information access and library collections. At the same time, faculty members must recognize the complexity of the problem and the inadequacy of simple solutions. Faculty must become more knowledgeable about the economic, technological, and legal aspects of scholarly publishing and more aware of the driving forces in this environment. They must be helped to understand how economic forces motivate the actions of publishers, the library, the university and, most importantly, their own actions as scholars. Most important, faculty must recognize that the challenge is one of choosing a future and not simply a problem of inadequate resources or faulty distributions of funds. Institutional funds are, for the most part, fungible and money spent on library resources is, therefore, money that could also be spent on laboratory equipment, faculty travel, and faculty salaries. In essence, the faculty must be asked to join with the library and other institutional agencies in making choices among competing options.

Encouraging faculty collaboration is crucial to the success of effective change management. However, in the end it is not the faculty's job to build library collections. If research universities are to be successful, each member of the university's staff must concentrate on the tasks that he or she is most qualified to do. For faculty, that is the direction of research, instruction, and service activities. Library staff, for their part, are most qualified to build collections and select information services. In our view, the process we have described will have been successful when the faculty demonstrate confidence that library staff will work effectively and efficiently within the broad guidelines that, collaboratively, we have generated. Even then, however, the faculty must be constantly informed about the status of collections, collection budgets, and developing modes of access so that they recognize the dynamic nature of these issues. Library staff and faculty together must redouble their efforts to understand the economics of information; to treat scholarly information and information access as one of many possible strategic investments in learning, research, and service; and to assure that investments in collections and information service repay the institution in the advancement of its mission. In today's dynamic environment, successful change management in research libraries and research universities is the proper framing and resolution of choices.

NOTES

1. Slaughter and Leslie also point out that global competitiveness has forced nations to divert funds from the social sector, including education, to the commercial to

protect and enhance the global competitiveness of the commercial sector. See Sheila Slaughter and Larry L. Leslie, *Academic Capitalism: Politics, Policies and the Entrepreneurial University* (Baltimore: Johns Hopkins University Press, 1997), 13-16.

2. The authors, while uncertain of first attribution, are certain that this anthropomorphic and iconic mantra predates even ancient Alexandria.

3. Federal programs have supported the acquisition of foreign library materials. A section of Public Law 480, for example, passed in 1961, provided funding for library materials from certain foreign countries in exchange for American foreign aid. Another program designed to promote the acquisition of foreign library materials was the Farmington Plan, a voluntary cooperative undertaking in which participating research libraries aspired to acquire and catalog "every book and pamphlet, published anywhere in the world following the effective date of the agreement, that might reasonably be expected to have interest to a research worker in America." Cf. Keyes Metcalf, "The Farmington Plan," *Harvard Library Bulletin* 2 (1948): 296.

4. "ARL data for 1996/97 show that, while ARL libraries more than doubled expenditures for serials from 1986 to 1997, they purchased 6% fewer serial subscriptions. During the last decade, libraries shifted expenditures from monographs to serials to meet some of the demands of increasing serial prices, reducing the number of monographs purchased by 14%, while the unit cost for monographs increased by 62%. Since 1986, the annual average increase for the serial unit cost has been 9.4% and for the monograph unit cost 4.5%, both higher than the general inflation trends in North America during the same period." Cf. Julia Blixrud, "Still Paying More; Still Getting Less," *ARL: A Bimonthly Newsletter of Research Library Issues and Actions* 199 (August 1998), http://www.arl.org/newsltr/199/still.html (10 March 1999).

5. Brian L. Hawkins, "The Unsustainability of the Traditional Library and the Threat to Higher Education," in *The Mirage of Continuity: Reconfiguring Academic Information Resources for the 21st Century*, ed. Brian L. Hawkins and Patricia Battin (Washington, D.C.: Council on Library and Information Resources and the American Association of Universities, 1998), 135.

6. Fiske and Hammond report that a "university's investment in technology and attention to new forms of teaching are often barometers of its curricular innovations and devotion to quality." See Edward Fiske and Bruce Hammond, "Identifying Quality in American Colleges and Universities" in *Planning for Higher Education* 26 (Fall 1997): 12.

7. "The descriptive handle that most readily attaches to the rising cost of scholarly publication is 'the library problem'–a seemingly permanent imbalance between the funds accorded to research libraries and the volume of scholarly output these libraries are expected to purchase and manage." Cf. "To Publish and Perish," *Policy Perspectives* 7 (March 1998): 1.

8. Leon Litwack, *op. cit.* in Author note.

9. Based on 1997 data reported by 110 members of the Association of Research Libraries (www.arl.org), Berkeley ranks 4th in number of volumes held, 7th in net volumes added, 4th in total number of current serials, 6th in total materials expenditures, and 7th in total library expenditures. It is interesting to note that Berkeley also ranks 55th in total number of teaching faculty, 13th in number of full-time graduate students, and 19th in total number of full-time students. Using the ratio of net vol-

umes added to total teaching faculty, Berkeley ranks 7th; using the ratio of total current serials to total teaching faculty, Berkeley ranks 2nd; and using the ratio of total materials expenditures to total teaching faculty, Berkeley ranks 14th.

10. Richard M. Doherty and Carol Hughes, *Preferred Futures for Libraries: A Summary of Six Workshops with University Provosts and Library Directors* (Mountain View, Ca.: Research Libraries Group, 1991): 5-6.

11. "Ownership and Access in a Global Information Market: A Framework for the University of Connecticut Libraries." http://www.lib.uconn.edu.

12. See, for instance, Craig Swenson, "Customers and Markets: The Cuss Words of Academe," Change 30 (Sept./Oct. 1998): 34-39.

13. Cf. Robert Zemsky and William F. Massey, "Toward an Understanding of Our Current Predicaments: Expanding Perimeters, Melting Cores, and Sticky Functions," *Change* 27 (Nov.-Dec. 1995): 40-49.

14. See Mark J. McCabe, "The Impact of Publisher Mergers on Journal Prices: A Preliminary Report," *ARL: A Bimonthly Newsletter of Research Library Issues and Actions* 200 (Oct. 1998): 3.

15. One example of an organized effort to focus library investment on more sustainable publishing models is ARL's SPARC project. Cf. Mary M. Case, "ARL Promotes Competition through SPARC: The Scholarly Publishing & Academic Resources Coalition," *ARL: A Bimonthly Newsletter of Research Library Issues and Actions* 196 (Feb. 1998): 1-5.

Budgeting for Collection Development in the Electronic Environment

Frederick C. Lynden

INTRODUCTION

The management of a collection budget in the electronic era is much more challenging than ever before. Budgets have three requirements:

1. They should be an estimate, often itemized, of expected income and expense;
2. They should be a plan of operation based upon such an estimate;
3. They should serve as an estimated allotment of funds for a given period.

On the other hand, electronic materials defy these requirements:

1. These materials have such a variety of payment plans that it is hard to estimate what expense they will cause;
2. These materials demand peripheral support which makes it difficult to develop a plan of operation without that support in place;
3. These materials are being published without much advance notice and are also politically sensitive since they decrease funds available for other formats.

Libraries are meeting these challenges through a variety of means, many of which will be mentioned today and tomorrow. In this paper, the Brown Library experience in purchasing electronic services will serve as a model for

Frederick C. Lynden is Associate Librarian, Technical Services, Brown University, Providence, RI.

[Haworth co-indexing entry note]: "Budgeting for Collection Development in the Electronic Environment." Lynden, Frederick C. Co-published simultaneously in *Journal of Library Administration* (The Haworth Information Press, an imprint of The Haworth Press, Inc.) Vol. 28, No. 4, 1999, pp. 37-56; and: *Collection Development in the Electronic Environment: Shifting Priorities* (ed: Sul H. Lee) The Haworth Information Press, an imprint of The Haworth Press, Inc., 1999, pp. 37-56. Single or multiple copies of this article are available for a fee from The Haworth Document Delivery Service [1-800-342-9678, 9:00 a.m. - 5:00 p.m. (EST). E-mail address: getinfo@haworthpressinc.com].

the issues of budgeting for electronic materials. In order to understand the environment in which the Brown University Library operates, it is necessary to describe this environment and outline the budgetary process.

Brown University is a Ivy League university of medium size. The current student body is close to 7,800; 5,200 undergraduates, 1,300 graduates, and 300 medical students. As a private institution, Brown depends heavily upon tuition which, for undergraduates, is currently $23,616. With room, board and fees the total cost per annum is $31,060. Because of its high tuition Brown has been seeking to lower the cost rise and this year's undergraduate tuition and fees rose only 3.9%. The average financial aid package is $21,777 and 37% of Brown undergraduates receive financial aid packages which include University grants. (Financial aid always competes with library funds for priority.)

There are seven libraries at Brown, the primary, open stack Rockefeller and Sciences libraries, the John Hay Library, the Orwig Music Library, the Demography Library, the Art Slide Library and the independent John Carter Brown Library, which holds a preeminent collection of Americana. These libraries now hold over three million volumes plus more than two million additional materials such as microforms, sheet music, compact discs, manuscripts, phonorecords, maps, art slides, electronic files, and other formats.

The annual expenditures for the Libraries, not including the John Carter Brown, were $13,844,816 in 1997/98. With the John Carter Brown Library added, the library expenditure at Brown in 1997/98 was about $14.4 million. The total university Educational and General expenditures in 1997/98 were $252,167,577. Thus, the libraries received 5% of the university dollars. In 1997/98, the Library expended $4,774,273 for Acquisitions and the total electronic expenditures were $348,501 or 7.3% of the Acquisitions budget. In the previous year, the total expenditures for electronic materials were $316,702 compared with Acquisition expenditures of $5,087,773 or 6.23%. The projected electronic expenditures for 1998/99 are $423,907 from an Acquisitions budget of $4,921,505 or 8.6%. Thus, electronic materials are taking an increasing share of the Acquisition budget which is shrinking the available monies for other formats.

BUDGETING PROCESS AT BROWN

Each fall the University asks the Library for a projection of the costs for the following fiscal year which at Brown runs from July 1 to June 30. This fall, for example, the University will be requesting data for the fiscal year 1999/2000. There is a university-wide hearing committee called the Advisory Committee on University Planning or ACUP which hears budget requests from throughout the campus. The ACUP group includes the Provost, other administration officials, professors and students. The Library is frequently asked to make a presentation before ACUP on the budget areas which have the highest inflation. As any librarian knows, with the inflation of serials, double digit increases have been the rule. As a result, there has often been a presentation to ACUP on inflation for Acquisitions. As early as 1994/95, ACUP, tired of hearing about double digit inflation in materials, made the following recommendation:

> Library Acquisitions: ACUP recommends adding $130,000 for library books and periodicals. While the Committee recognizes this is not enough to keep pace with inflation, it also acknowledges the futility of matching annual double digit inflationary increases for books and periodicals. ACUP supports all efforts to enhance access to library materials through non-traditional means such as electronic services and intercollegiate sharing. (1)

This reasoning was both far sighted and short sighted. As librarians well know, electronic services and intercollegiate sharing do vastly improve access, but they are also aware that the infrastructure and administrative apparatus required to make such access available is not economical. Indeed, it can frequently cost more than paper products and is more often than not impermanent.

Once the Library budget has been submitted, the University administration reviews it, the administration looks at the ACUP proposals, and then submits it to the Corporation or the Board of Trustees. The Corporation then makes its recommendations and in the spring the Library receives its budget. If the Library is dissatisfied, then it can make a case for special funds from the Provost or President. The budget is finalized in late May and is ready for spending on July 1.

POLITICS OF BUDGETING

The Brown University Library has been quite successful in the politics of budgeting. For example, the last three acquisition budgets showed additions by either the President or ACUP due to efforts on the part of the University Librarian. For example, the following amounts were added to the budget:

- 1996/97: $200,000 (President)
- 1997/98: $250,000 (President)
- 1998/99: $190,000 (ACUP) (amount added to the base)

The efforts on the part of the University Librarian were based upon the internal budgeting process at Brown which illustrates how an open budgeting process can provide eye-opening data for the University Administration. Usually a strong argument for increases comes from the process of allocating the acquisitions budget.

The memo from the University Librarian to the Provost talks about two major issues: a memo from the Acquisitions Group on cuts to acquisition program necessary due to the limited increase and the possibility of emergency one-time funding from the President. Further, Merrily Taylor speaks briefly about electronic resources: "Community demand for electronic resources increases annually . . . these resources not only do not save money or displace existing print demand, but they constitute an entirely new format for scholarly publication which cannot be ignored." (2) She goes on to note: "To continue to apply 1% increases to the Acquisitions budget in this environment is to doom the Library collections, print and electronic, to steady, relentless erosion, and to prevent the kind of growth and development which is essential to support both traditional and new academic programs." (3)

In this particular request, in addition to this effort to fund new formats, the University Librarian leans heavily on the issue of irrational and unpredictable annual support and asks the Provost to work together with her on a formula which would assure the Library of "some reasonable, predictable annual support for the acquisition budget. With such support, we can undoubtedly produce annual giving and new endowment income which will do much to pick up the slack. Without it, any fulsome visions of 'the Library of the future' might as well be put on the shelf, since the Library *of the present* will not be able to meet its obligations." (4)

In this instance, the University Librarian attached a memo on the cuts necessary to achieve a balance including a major cut in Serials, a dramatic reduction in Special Collections, no new electronic products, elimination of binding of paperback books, a cancellation of Brown's membership in the Center for Research Libraries, etc. These were all very distasteful reductions.

OPEN BUDGET PROCESS

There are many participants in the development of the Acquisition Budget: In addition to the University Librarian, a principal participant is the Library Business Manager who receives the budget documents from the University. She, in turn, transmits this information to the Acquisition Department Head who makes up the first allocation proposal in conference with the Head Serials Librarian, the Head of Collection Development, and the Associate University Librarian for Public Services and Collection Development.

The initial allocation document is a key element in the budgeting process (Appendix 1). It includes the available budget: Library Appropriation (General Funds); Endowment; Medical Funds; and Cash (Gift funds and transfers). The document also includes a history of the previous year, what was allocated and what was expended. Next it covers the same categories with a projection. Then, there is a column for reductions since the projected amount never matches the available budget. Finally, the adjusted column covers the final amount set for the year's work. Notes always explain how certain figures were derived.

The actual process of setting the projected amounts needed for monographs and serials includes looking at past history of expenditures and projections on price increases by vendors as well as data from the Library Materials Price Index Committee of ALA. The first projections are for serials (Head, Serials Librarian), the Approval plans (Head, Acquisitions), and Disciplines (Head, Collection Development and Head, Acquisitions). Special Collections has a formula of 5% of the General Funds + Endowments + Gifts (restricted to Special Collections). The medical budget comes from the School of Medicine in consultation with the AUL for Public Services and Collection Development and the Medical Coordinator. Other elements depend upon staff associated with these categories, e.g., Bindery budget is derived by the Head, Preservation Department in consultation with the binder; the Documents budget, by the Documents Coordinator, etc. In 1998/99 no monies were set aside for new electronic materials (most current electronic materials are purchased from the serials budget and are broken out under the Serials line). The lack of a line for new electronic materials has not prevented expenditures for current electronic materials.

The above staff then attempt to cut the estimates to the size of the budget. This requires participation by all parties. This discussion is useful to all participants as well as to the University Librarian who receives a final report from the Associate University Librarian for Technical Services who sets up the meeting and insures the reports are done.

The Serials estimate is always very crucial to the Acquisitions budget (Appendix 2). Prepared by Steven E. Thompson, Head, Serials Department, this estimate has most often been right on target. In the past couple of years, with the strengthening of the dollar, there has been a surplus despite its great accuracy in previous years. Therefore, due to demands on the budget this year, the Serials estimate was reduced as part of the allocation process which includes much negotiation. It was decided that, if in the spring when most of the serial invoices have been received, the allocation was inadequate, then the University Librarian would go to the Provost for emergency help. To date, the 11% estimate has been far too high. Among the usual stocking horses for major price increases are foreign publishers. In 1998/99, for Brown's mix of titles, however, Elsevier has had price increases at a 4% level; Kluwer at 5%; and Springer at 7%. The true gougers this year are Academic at 18% and Wiley at 22%. The overall increase for periodicals is at a 6% level.

The electronic serials estimate uses a base calculated from historical data, new products, additions to First Search (an OCLC composite of electronic databases), transfers from discipline funds, and savings from early payments (Appendix 3). The base for this category is $385,370. With an inflationary increase of 10%, the midpoint of many vendors' projected range for serial price increases, which adds $38,537, the total comes to $423,907. The actual invoices coming in or expected to come in amount to $396,202, or an amount within 5% of the estimated costs.

The end product of the allocation process is sometimes a cutback in the estimated cost or sometimes an over allocation of a limited amount which can usually be covered at year's end by gift receipts. The allocation process has served Brown very well. Not only does it acquaint staff from a variety of areas about the Acquisitions Budget but it also serves as a political tool which can be used to persuade the University Administration of library needs. Further it provides a historical record of budgets and costs. For the first time, a breakdown of electronic serial costs was included last year in the serials line. Many faculty are interested to know how much the Library spends on electronic materials.

EDUCATION OF USERS

Brown has employed a variety of means to keep the University administration, faculty, and donors apprised of the Acquisition Budget. First, ACUP is always informed about the projected increases in the costs of monographs, serials, and binding. Second, since 1996 the Library has prepared an annual promotional brochure on Endowment funds. This is mailed to donors, faculty with endowed chairs, and the University administration. In 1997, the Library report was entitled "Keeping Pace with Technology" (5) and it honored specifically those donors who made possible the electronic infrastructure at the Brown Library. For example, it mentioned gifts from a Brown alumnus and a foundation which made possible the completion of retrospective conversion. In the same issue, it spoke about the donation which made possible the Laura and Alfred Hecker Center for Library Technology which is a learning center "theater" in the Library at Brown which has 20 sophisticated PC's with a teaching console for projecting images on a screen and permits staff to train patrons on using the latest electronic tools. With pictures of technology headed by the title: "Gifts Advance the Library's Technology," this promotional brochure gave emphasis to the electronic revolution in Libraries. It also noted:

> The recognition that some of Brown's collections are centuries old is a
> vivid counterpoint to the realization that electronic media are not as

enduring as print that there is an ephemeral quality about a slender CD and an intangible database. Print, and in some cases, microform, remains the most reliable form in which to preserve knowledge for the distant future. For the moment at least, the Library must acquire electronic resources not as replacements for, but in addition to print collections and often at a higher cost. (6)

Third, in another educational venture, the Library participated in a university-wide strategic planning process. The University Librarian served as a member of the Task Force on Information Resources and Support. Each Task Force produced recommendations for improvements. The Provost then asked each department to prepare mini-proposals outlining the budgetary needs. The Library prepared a mini-proposal on the acquisitions budget which requested the university to:

- Increase the Library's Information Resources Budget annually in excess of the increases scheduled for the rest of the operating budget.
- Treat income from all new endowments as incremental.
- Allow the Library to draw on its acquisition endowments at a rate greater than that used for all other endowments in the University.

In the presentation on the first request to increase the Information Resources budget, there was a line about electronic materials: " . . . we have been unable to acquire many new serials and other resources which faculty and students have requested, while the publication of material in electronic formats places further demands on the budget." (7) An immediate result of the first request was an addition of $190,000 to the Library's base budget. The second request has now been assured and the Library does not hope to achieve the third and last request.

Fourth, in an effort to promote the Library collections, the Library participated in a celebration of the acquisition of the 3 millionth volume during the spring meeting of the Corporation. There was a dinner in Providence and a viewing of "water fires" on one of the waterways in Providence. This was an opportunity to inform Board of Trustees members about Library needs. In a brochure prepared for the celebration, the Brown Library described three gifts received from an alumnus to celebrate the 3 millionth volume. One of the three gifts was a group of on-line databases from Chadwyck Healy. Named in honor of the donor, the Paul R. Dupee Jr. '65 Digital Reference Collections, the LION (Literature On-line) databases were described in this brochure. (8)

Finally, in order to obtain funding from both the Provost and the Medical School for an electronic collection called the Web of Science, the Associate University Librarian for Public Services and Collection Development held an informational session at the Hecker Center for Medical School and Sciences faculty and wrote to both the Provost and the Associate Dean of the Medical School appealing for assistance. The Provost offered a total of $135,366 for three academic years, and the Medical School provided $67,683. Thus, over $200,000 will go towards the payment for this major electronic index.

BUDGETING FOR ELECTRONIC MATERIALS

One of the major issues in budgeting for electronic materials is the variety of payment plans offered by the publishers of electronic materials. The Library Materials Price Index Committee (LMPIC) of the Association for Library Collections and Technical Services of the American Library Association has decided to forego price indexes for electronic materials for the foreseeable future due to the difficulties of tracking and indexing these types of materials. This decision was based on a report entitled: LMPIC Report on Electronic Products Price Tracking, June 29, 1997. This report by Penny Schroeder, Frederick Lynden, and Marifran Bustion is divided into four sections which cover various barriers to getting precise price information: Availability Issues; Access Issues; Consortia Issues; and Other Issues. (9) These issues prevent standard reporting of prices because individual institutions have different pricing schedules based on a variety of parameters.

Availability Issues

First, until recently most publishers have *required* libraries to subscribe to the *paper copy* before being able to obtain the electronic version. Now there are some variations. For example, Highwire Marketing Group has a special price list for institutions. There are these categories: Print Only, Print Plus On-line (Bundled), and On-line Only. (10)

Second, there can be a variety of surcharges to obtain *different versions*. For example, a surcharge can be added to the print to obtain the electronic or vice-versa, a surcharge to the electronic to obtain the print.

Third, there are also different prices for *different formats*, e.g., one price for the CD-ROM version, another for print, and another for on-line access. See the Highwire list.

Fourth, often an electronic product is part of a total package *(bundled) plan* and it is hard to isolate the specific cost of the electronic version. For example, Springer Verlag offers an electronic version *free* with any subscription to a print version. However, they do not show a separate cost for each version but instead have increased the overall price to cover the costs of the electronic version. (11)

Fifth, variations exist between *full and partial text* versions. EBSCOhost, in its Academic search fullText elite, has full text for some titles and only abstracts and indexing for others. Each vendor offering such a selection of titles has a different proportion of full and partial text titles. (12)

Sixth, often libraries must purchase an entire bundled *package* of titles rather than individual titles. Elsevier offers very few electronic titles individually. They prefer that you purchase their package ScienceDirect. (13)

Seventh, prices may be computed according to the *years of coverage*. For example, in order to obtain backfiles of the Web of Science, it was necessary to pay different fees for different time spans. (14)

Eighth, costs vary according to the *type of product*, database, or electronic journal. A recent title called the *Collection of Czechoslovak Chemical Communications* has the following types of subscriptions : (1) Print Only ($518) (2) Print and Web ($518) (3) Web only ($492) (4) CD only ($518) (5) CD and Web ($518) (6) Print and CD ($549) and (7) Print and CD and Web ($549). This is published by an Institute of Organic Chemistry and Biochemistry of the Academy of Sciences of the Czech Republic. (15)

Ninth, prices are reckoned according to the *image version* of an electronic product, e.g., whether ASCII or bit mapped images.

Access Issues

First, the publisher can determine the *location of usage*, i.e., where a product will be used. For example, Wiley defines a site as "a single geographically contiguous office building or complex or campus location plus dial-in access via the Licensee's secure network, identified by the Licensee's relevant Internet Protocol (I.P.) addresses, for Users as defined below . . . " (16)

Second, prices may be based on the *number of simultaneous users* or the number of ports requested. For example, prices for Harrison's On-line, a database of medical information from McGraw-Hill, depend upon the number of users using the product. The price for 5 simultaneous users is $875 and $1,250 for 10 simultaneous users. (17)

Third, prices may be calculated based upon the number of *passwords* issued, the *size of the acquisition budget*, or *dollars spent with a publisher*.

Fourth, there may be additional charges for *printing or downloading*. For example, "if a search of the database finds an article from a Psychology Press journal that the institution does not subscribe to, a charge will be made for delivery of this article. We offer a convenient and simple way of prepaying for the retrieval of such 'non-subscribed' articles: a 10 article subscription to the Electronic Journal. On purchase of such a subscription at £100 or $160, an institution will be allowed to retrieve and deliver to the desks of individuals within the institution any 10 articles in the database." (18)

Fifth, prices may be computed according to whether the product is *networked or stands alone*, the *number of transactions*, the *number of users or FTE's*.

Sixth, *interlibrary loan rights* may be restricted. The license for American Society of Microbiology states: "no material from any ASM Journal On-line may be used for fee-for-service purposes, such as document delivery services." (19)

Seventh, there can be *special conditions* regarding backfiles or prior usage. As noted above, the Web of Science charges for backfiles at different rates for different periods. ISI, which publishes Web of Science, also has a complicated discount schedule depending upon your print copies. Some publishers charge for prior usage with an extra percent.

Consortia Issues

First, *prices* can *vary* depending upon the consortium. The Consortium of Rhode Island Academic and Research Libraries (CRIARL) has an offer from Academic Press which requires a three-year term with automatic annual renewals thereafter. For the IDEAL collection from Academic a consortium can have a collection of one or more of AP's 175 journals. Each of the libraries, depending upon its size, has a different price. However, the pricing is a complicated mix of discounts for print titles and fees for electronic subscriptions which one has to calculate on a title by title basis. (20) ISI's Web of Science consortial subscription, however, from NERL (Northeast Regional Libraries), has one price for every library whether it be Yale or Brown. This, of course, can be a disadvantage for smaller libraries.

Second, *subscription conditions* change. Consortia libraries may be forced to purchase total bundled packages of titles at first. Later they may be able to customize purchases. Another situation can occur. Some titles may be dropped during a year. Many libraries have purchased packages from UMI or EBSCO to discover later that certain titles are no longer available.

Other Issues

Product characteristics. There may be overlap of titles offered by different providers and package deals can cause duplication. The size of a package can vary tremendously. The American Chemical Society for example has a variety of different packages. Often electronic products require specific and/or proprietary equipment or software to be fully used.

Ownership. Confusion exists over exactly what a library owns. In Beilstein's standard agreement, there is a provision that all the files return to Beilstein once the agreement is terminated and backfiles are sometimes, and sometimes not, included. (21)

Lack of stable price lists. Of course, different prices are negotiated for different libraries sometimes without relation to the print. Secrecy is a problem since a contract may prohibit disclosure of the exact price. Cost varies on the mix of titles and dealing directly with publishers frequently causes complications in price tracking. (22)

MEANS FOR TRACKING ELECTRONIC PRODUCT PRICES

Clearly, the obstacles to tracking prices, making estimates, and budgeting for electronic materials are many. This paper will propose some means of coming up with budgetary estimates. However, they have many pitfalls and they can be costly as well. It is clear that comparisons are practically impossible. It seems as if libraries have temporarily at least, and not by choice, returned to the Wild West of Acquisitions when libraries went directly to publishers and vendors did not have large segments of the market. It is simply the case that many publishers do not offer their products through vendors. However, this situation is changing.

1. Local Library Estimates. Currently using a local library system is the best means of getting a handle on what electronic materials cost. There is one caveat, however, when the print and electronic versions are bundled with one price; there is no way possible to get precise price information. Nevertheless, it is possible to tag all purchases with a code which indicates whether or not the item is an electronic journal, an electronic database, or a CD-ROM. These purchases can then be aggregated and a total cost can be established for each year. The year to year progression can then be followed to see what the change is.

There were two major problems with this accounting of Brown's expenditures. First, there are currently so many additions to the list of titles that it is hard to track inflation. Second, a number of titles have backfiles which also distort the progression of costs. Despite these drawbacks, this is currently one of the few ways to follow the progression of costs. The percentage of expenditures can be of value when faculty ask how much of the Acquisition (Information Resources) budget is being used for electronic information. It is important to be able to answer this question which often comes from disgruntled Social Sciences and Humanities faculty. Unfortunately, there were very few titles to compare year to year because of product changes or bundling of costs with the print version.

2. Working with Vendors to Track Expenditures. Currently, there are a number of vendors with systems to supply electronic materials. Blackwell Publishing mentions, in a recent flyer, the major vendors supplying electronic materials (23):

- Blackwell Electronic Journal Navigator
- Dawson Information Quest

- EBSCO On-line
- SWETSNET

These vendors like to call themselves aggregators. They provide an on-line database with the various products (i.e., if they have a contract with publishers). They order the item and send you the license. They also let you know what titles offer an electronic version as part of the price. Clearly, they can provide comparative price data if they have it. Kathleen Born from EBSCO sent data on the number of electronic titles EBSCO handles (24):

- February 1997–850
- February 1998–2,200
- February 1999–3,600

As can be seen, the number is growing rapidly. The only difficulty with opting for one aggregator is that if a Library does not subscribe to a title from the aggregator then, in most cases, it is necessary to pay a fee, thus adding to the expense. Aggregators are also unable to inform their customers about the costs of the electronic materials if these materials are bundled together with the paper version. According to Ms. Born again:

> EBSCO receives price lists from publishers beginning in July/August each year. The publisher lists the prices for each version of their title. For example, print + on-line = $xx; on-line only = $xx; print only = $xx. If the electronic title is priced by number of users or full time students, we list all of the pricing options so the customer knows the amount they must pay and our orders and checks are correct to the publisher. (25)

However, it is possible to get from vendors comparative price data on the titles handled by them where there is a separate electronic price (and the library concerned orders an on-line version). The advantage is obviously having a single source for multiple electronic products.

3. Ordering Through a Bibliographic Utility. At the moment there is only one Bibliographic Utility which offers to supply libraries with electronic materials although OCLC works through vendors and publishers. OCLC provides services through OCLC FirstSearch Electronic Collections On-line. As do the other vendors, OCLC offers searching and browsing. There are some unique services. OCLC links electronic journals with FirstSearch databases; and it promises to archive all the titles held through EOC. Another service which EOC offers is consortia accounts. "EOC supports consortia purchasing which lets you share access to a common group of journals with other libraries while you continue to add journals that only your user may access." (26)

4. Adding a Position for Electronic Services. With all of the complicated purchasing options and the legal questions involved in examining licenses, many libraries are hiring staff simply to deal with electronic services. The University of Virginia posted a position for a Digital Acquisitions Coordinator who would report to the Director of the Acquisitions and Preservation Department. The position description notes:

> Coordinates acquisition of all digital library materials; manages licenses and contracts related to digital acquisitions; and works with collection managers and subject selectors, library systems staff, and University Purchasing agents to facilitate access and contract issues. The Coordinator is responsible for communication about digital materials within the Library and university, negotiating with vendors, monitoring trends in electronic publishing and licensing . . . (27)

MIT has also added such a position recently. Clearly, with a staff member specifically responsible for digital materials, it would be possible to monitor expenditures and prepare improved budgets for this area.

These are just some of the ways which libraries can use to better cope with the tracking of the costs of electronic resources.

PLANNING FOR ELECTRONIC SERVICES

As noted in the introduction, planning is a key element in budgeting for electronic services. At Brown, planning for the purchase of electronic resources is vested in a committee called the Electronic Resources and Services Committee (ERSC). This committee consists of the Associate University Librarian for Public Services and Collection Development, the Head of Systems, the Head of Serials, the Head of Reference, the Assistant Head of Reference, the Documents Coordinator, and the Head of Collection Development. Recently, they have added the Director, Scholarly Communication and Library Research and the Head of Cataloging. At a typical meeting they discuss potential resources and their cost, licensing issues, cataloging issues, technical issues, and policies for acquiring electronic resources.

A product of this library-wide committee is the "Brown University Library Electronic Resource Request Form." In addition to the usual information for purchasing such as author, title, publisher, selector, funds to be charged, the request form asks about whether or not the same product exists in another form; can we cancel, store or withdraw the other version (budgetary implications); accessibility/service level and costs (one-time and ongoing); preferred tier of service (Slide); system requirements; implementation analysis, i.e., impact on various departments, e.g., collection development, systems, reference, cataloging, acquisitions/serials, ERSC, and others; license agreement; approval recommendation (from faculty and staff) and electronic product implementation checklist (ordering, cataloging, cgi scripts, demo for staff, handout, public workstations, links on Web, problem reporting contact person, announcement to user, and other). The last requirement has date to be completed, by whom, and actual completion date. Another recent product of this group was Guidelines for Selection of ELIBRARY2 CD-ROM Products.

Another aspect of planning is outreach to the faculty to inform them about resources and to discover their interests. To this date, there have been meetings with the Departmental Library Representatives (faculty who represent their department to the Library) from seven science departments: Applied Math, Biology and Medicine, Chemistry, Engineering, Geology, Mathematics, and Physics. The meetings have been set up by the Associate University Librarian for Technical Services and have included the Head of Collection Development, the Serials Librarian, the Selector for the discipline and the Associate University Librarian for Public Services and Collection Development. Departments have invited all interested faculty. The pros and cons of electronic materials have been discussed at each meeting. Further, faculty are acquainted with what is available in their field. Brown has used some convenient lists from the University of Pennsylvania and Princeton to inform the faculty about what is available. These presentations have been highly successful. The faculty member from Physics wrote Steve E. Thompson, Head of the Serial Department at the Brown University Library:

> Thank you so much for all your help which has resulted in so many and such speedy successes in spite of rather fuzzy help from the publishers. I look forward to the era when it all settle down but is certainly fun now (at least for us the readers)! (28)

This particular professor has maintained contact with the Library regarding electronic materials becoming available, news about electronic publications from the *N.Y. Times,* etc.

It is incumbent upon librarians to publicize electronic resources otherwise they may be invisible. Brown has a policy to catalog all resources and put the name of the title on the Web as well. There are links between the catalog record and the Web site of the product.

The above types of activities, a planning group and contact with faculty, are necessary to the entire budgeting process since purchase of electronic products requires an infrastructure and the impact of the purchase must be known in order to budget for that infrastructure.

CONCLUSION

The Brown experience with budgeting for electronic materials is both positive and negative. There are a number of positive outcomes of the efforts to increase and improve electronic resources at Brown:

First, the Library has been able to budget for an increasing number of electronic resources without a separate fund by using an inflationary projection for electronic serials.

Second, the Library has been able to acquire exceptionally expensive titles through political efforts, e.g., contacting appropriate departments and/or the University administration regarding the need for these materials as well as memberships in consortia.

Third, the Library has been able to track gross electronic expenditures by using expense codes in its on-line acquisition system.

Fourth, the Library has administrative devices in place to insure that the proper infrastructure is available for electronic materials, e.g., ERSC.

Fifth, the Library has made it clear to the university administration and faculty that electronic resources are not a panacea which will replace print paper products or other media, or that electronic materials will provide cost savings for the Library in the long run.

There are also some challenges which Brown has not been able to overcome:

First, the Library has had to make tradeoffs in order to obtain electronic materials. For example, the agreement with ISI has discounts for print versions. The Library is saving on the annual cost by not purchasing the current print version of something available electronically.

Second, it is still not possible for the library to track specific costs for electronic materials because the publishers' bundling system only permits a tracking of gross expenditures. For example, until publishers unbundle costs for electronic materials, it will not be possible to come up with projections based upon the history of electronic expenditures.

Third, the interpretation of and revisions to licenses is still a very burdensome task for which Brown does not have adequate staff or training. Brown has asked a current staff member to provide this expertise but training will still be necessary.

Fourth, it is unclear whether or not the Library will begin to lose its access to materials for which there is no archiving. This is a serious problem of all electronic materials from which Brown is not able to protect itself.

Fifth, as noted above, the Library cannot continue to purchase electronic materials without shifting costs from print materials and there are political issues here which the Library must overcome. Some predict that in three to five years, prices will be unbundled. At the moment, publishers consider this too risky and many librarians are reluctant to purchase materials which may not be permanent, either because they will be technologically out-of-date or the contract removes them from a library once it expires.

Budgeting for electronic materials is in its infancy and there are still many challenges to meet.

ENDNOTES

1. "Special Report: Budget Recommendations for 1994-95," *George Street Journal* 18:7 (February 11, 1994).

2. Memo from Merrily E. Taylor, University Librarian, to the Provost of Brown University, September 15, 1997 re the 1997/98 Acquisition Budget.

3. *Ibid.*

4. *Ibid.*

5. *Keeping Pace with Technology: a Report Honoring Those who Have Given to the Brown University Library and the John Carter Brown Library*, Providence, Brown University, 1997, 20 p.

6. *Ibid.*, p. 4.

7. "IR 7, 8, 9: Relating to the Library Information Resources (Acquisitions) Budget, Paper of 14 October, 1997.

8. *Three for Three Million: The Paul R. Dupee Jr. '65 Acquisitions Celebrating the Brown University Library's Three Millionth Volume,* Office of the University Librarian, Brown University Library, Box A, Providence, RI 02912 [October 1977], 20 p.

9. "Library Materials Price Index Committee Report on Electronic Products Price Tracking," June 29, 1997, a paper by Frederick Lynden, Penny Schroeder, and Marifran Bustion.

10. Highwire Marketing Group, "Pricing for Institutions" <http://hwmg.stanford.edu/prices.html>

11. Springer. Customer Service. "Link Alert" <http://link.springer.de/alert/>

12. EBSCOhost <http://www.epnet.com/host/login.html>

13. Elsevier. Science Direct <http://www.sciencedirect.com>

14. "Web of Science, Brown University NERL Split Payment," Memo from Institute of Scientific Information to Brown University Library, June 1, 1998.

15. Letter from Institute of Organic Chemistry and Biochemistry, Academy of Science of the Czech Republic, Prague October 13, 1998 to Brown University Library.

16. Wiley Interscience, Basic Access License <http://www3.interscience.wiley.com/basic_license.html>

17. *Harrison's Online, License Agreement ("License") The McGraw-Hill Companies ("McGraw-Hill"),* 1999.

18. Psychology Online <http://www.tandf.co.uk/Psypress/psychonline.htm>

19. American Society for Microbiology, Institutional/Nonmember Online Site License Agreement for Full-Text Access <http://www.journals.asm.org/subscriptions/sitelicense.shtml>

20. The Academic Press Online Library, IDEAL (International Digital Electronic Access Library) <http://www.idealibrary.com> and 1997 Appeal Pricing–Rhode Island–All Inclusive, 11/12/97.

21. Beilstein Information Systems License Agreement, Section 10.7, 9/16/96.

22. This entire discussion benefited from an excellent article: Knight, Nancy H. and Susan B. Hillson, "Electronic Pubs Pricing in the web era," *Information Today* 15:8: 39-40 (May 1998).

23. Blackwell Publishers. Online Journals Information <http://www.blackwellpublishers.3co.uk/Static/online.htm>

24. Personal Communication from Kathleen Born, Director, Academic Division, EBSCO Subscription Services (ESS), Birmingham, AL, 18 Feb. 1999.

25. *Ibid.*

26. OCLC Electronic Collections Online. Service Overview <http://www.oclc.org/oclc.eco/service.thm#tools>

27. Posting for University of Virginia Library, Office of the Librarian, Faculty Opening, *Digital Acquisitions Coordinator*, October 21, 1998.

28. Memo to Steven Thompson from Robert E. Lanou, Jr., 25 Feb. 1998.

APPENDIX 1. 1998/99 Information Resources Budget–Final

AVAILABLE BUDGET=	$4,921,505					
LA	$3,515,314	includeds $190k added to base by ACUP for acquisitions and storage				
Endowment	$1,014,951					
Medicine	$374,375					
Cash	$16,865					

EXPENSES	1997/98 allocated	1997/98 expended	1998/99 projected	1998/99 reduction	1998/99 adjusted	NOTES
SERIALS	$2,835,000	$2,683,694	$2,606,935	$180,000	$2,426,935	
electronic products			$423,907		$423,907	
DeWitt Wallace			$6,964		$6,964	endowment restricted to serials
APPROVAL PLANS	$490,000	$499,183	$500,000	$50,000	$450,000	
SPECIAL COLL.	$237,362	$238,392	$284,990	$60,000	$224,990	projected=5% LA ($3,325,314)
Stamps	$22,916	$22,916	$25,273		$25,273	+ Endowments (Gifts+NEH not
ASK Brown	$3,935	$3,935	$6,079		$6,079	incl.) less $10,000 for payment
						made in FY 95/96; adjusted = LA
						– $60,000 or 3.02% of $3,515,314
DISCIPLINES	$390,000	$405,024	$430,000	$30,000	$400,000	expenditures includes cash funds
MEDICINE	$364,845	$349,017	$0	$0	$374,375	
(serials portion)		$334,525				
NEH	$50,333	$50,333	$50,333	0	$50,333	25% Spec Coll ($26,250) & 15%
						Art ($15,750) & $8,333 Hall-Hoag
BINDING	$180,000	$193,047	$208,499	$0	$208,490	8% increase
COLLECTION MAINT.	$10,000	$5,744	$10,000	$0	$10,000	
COURSE RESERVES	$22,000	$22,225	$23,350	$0	$23,350	5% increase
ELEC. PRODUCTS	$0	$0	$0	$0	$0	new products
EXCHANGES	$26,000	$25,451	$28,250	$0	$28,250	11% Increase
GOVT. DOCS.	$20,000	$22,598	$20,000	$0	$20,000	
LIBRARIAN	$8,334	$8,334	$8,334	$0	$8,334	Hall-Hoag
POSTAGE	$26,000	$29,368	$30,000	$0	$30,000	monographs only
SETS	$65,000	$56,369	$59,200	$10,000	$49,200	projected=5% incease; adjusted =
						less $10,000 in cancellations
OPERATING EXPENSES:						
DOC. DELIVERY	$24,000	$26,540	$25,000	$0	$25,000	portion to be covered by
						acquisitions budget
OCLC			$100,000	$50,000	$50,000	portion to be covered by
						acquisitions budget
NEH PRESERVATION			$11,259	$0	$20,025	income from NEH Preservation
						endowments
PRESERVATION	$10,000	$10,000	$10,000	$0	$10,000	income frrom NEH Preservation
						endowments
STORAGE	$50,000	$50,000	$50,000	$0	$50,000	portion to be covered by
						acquisitions budget
TOTALS	$4,835,725	$4,702,170	$4,918,364	$380,000	$4,921,505	$0

APPENDIX 2. Estimate of 1998/99 Serials Expenses

1997/98 Net Serials Expenditure	$2,683,694				
					SET 8/3/98
	Base Cost	Inflation Factor	Inflation Amount	1998/99 Estimate	Notes
Materials					
Prepaid Subscriptions	$2,062,111	11%	$226,832	$2,288,943	*11% U.S., UK, Eur.; $17,995 Transfers
Irregular Serials	$169,551	6.6%	$11,190	$180,741	$600 Transfers
Monographic Series	$135,317	10.8%	$14,614	$149,931	
Memberships	$88,817	10.5%	$9,326	$98,143	
Electronic Products	$385,370	10%	$38,537	$423,907	$14,500 Transfers
	$2,841,166	10.7%	$300,499	$3,141,665	
Estimate of Materials Expenses for 1998/99				**$3,141,665**	
Ancillary Charges					
Replacements				$5,000	
Service				$21,000	
Postage				$19,000	
Estimate of 1998/99 Total Serials Expenses				**$3,186,665**	
Credits					
Prepayment Credits				($46,982)	
1997/98 Rollover				($108,841)	
Total Credits				**($155,823)**	
Net Requirement for 1998/99 Serials Expenses				**$3,030,842**	

APPENDIX 3. 1998/99 Net Serials Expenses

Electronic Products Estimate:

    The Library subscribes to a number of electronic services such as FirstSearch, AcademicSearch, and JSTOR as well as CD-ROM products. Last year the cost of these services/material was $291,000. This year, the Library is adding the Web of Science for which the serials budget is allocating $85,000 (net increase is $36,000 as both Gmelin and ISI print indexes have been removed from the budget). Additionally, the FirstSearch service has been augmented and will cost an additional $9,000 and there are transfers from discipline funds of $6,000. Payment has already been made for the Avery and ESTC products for 1998/99 and consequently $5,630 is saved for this year. This makes the base for this category $385,370. An increase of 10% will be applied to this base for 1997/98. This will add $38,537.

                1998/99 Electronic Product Estimate   *$423,907*

Service Charges

    Service charges cover all postage costs (incl. shipping and handling, etc.) in addition to service charges. Last year's increase was 14% with postage charges and service charges sharing the increase almost equally. Last year's expenditure of $36,723 will be increased by $3,277 (8.9%) to bring the allocation to $40,000.

                1998/99 Service Charge Estimate   *$40,000*

Replacements

          The allocation of $5,000 remains the same.

                1998/99 Replacements   *$5,000*

Credits

    This year prepayments for 1999 subscriptions were made to EBSCO, Harrassowitz, Nijhoff, and Blackwell's. Estimated credit amounts that will be realized are: Harrassowitz $15,435; Blackwell's $12,516, Nijhoff $7,726, and EBSCO $11,305. Additionally, balances remain from last year's Harrassowitz, Blackwell, and Nijhoff prepayments which total $108,841.

                1998/99 Credits   *−$155,823*

1998/99 Serials Expenses

    The net total of $3,032,842 represents a 14.1% increase over the net 1997/98 LA serials expenditure of $2,683,694.

                1998/99 Serials Estimate   *$3,032,842*

                1998/99 Net Serials Expenses   *$3,030,842*

From Journal Cancellation
to Library Strategic Visioning
Faculty Leadership

Olivia M. A. Madison

It began as any other university journal cancellation project–Iowa State University (ISU) had gone through this difficult and painful experience three times before, with its first cancellation project being in 1980-81. As had happened before, the ISU Library's acquisitions expenditures were increasing at rates that exceeded available acquisitions funds.

During the late fall of 1997 through the spring of 1998, various library administrators had given presentations on the impending budget crisis to the University Library Committee, a committee composed of representatives from each college, two student governance organizations, the Computation Center, and the Faculty Senate. This process was not new to the library committee, as it had played important roles in the last three cancellation projects and by spring was well aware that a cancellation project was inevitable. The library administrators had provided the library committee with budget analyses over the past several years, all indicating the statistical inevitability of the current budget crisis. They asked the library committee for its advice on methodologies to use. For example, should the library institute across the board percentage cuts or consider differential percentage cuts by disciplines. How and when should the library involve the faculty in identifying journal titles to cancel? What information should be provided to the faculty for their best-informed decisions?

Based upon the library committee's input, the Dean of Library Services began the project in April 1998 with a formal announcement to the university

Olivia M. A. Madison is Dean of Library Services, Iowa State University Library.

[Haworth co-indexing entry note]: "From Journal Cancellation to Library Strategic Visioning Faculty Leadership." Madison, Olivia M. A. Co-published simultaneously in *Journal of Library Administration* (The Haworth Information Press, an imprint of The Haworth Press, Inc.) Vol. 28, No. 4, 1999, pp. 57-70; and: *Collection Development in the Electronic Environment: Shifting Priorities* (ed: Sul H. Lee) The Haworth Information Press, an imprint of The Haworth Press, Inc., 1999, pp. 57-70. Single or multiple copies of this article are available for a fee from The Haworth Document Delivery Service [1-800-342-9678, 9:00 a.m. - 5:00 p.m. (EST). E-mail address: getinfo@haworthpressinc.com].

57

community that a journal cancellation project would begin fall semester with a goal of a 14% cut in journal expenditures. In late February 1999, following two all-university reviews of proposed lists of journals to be cancelled, the final list of titles to be cancelled was listed on the library's Web pages. As such projects go, I could not have asked for a better library process and faculty involvement. The careful preliminary planning, coordinated and led by two different collections officers, was evident throughout the project. The project infrastructure included accurate title lists with journal costs, and a detailed Web page with frequently asked questions and links to other university library sites with information on their cancellation projects. In addition there was close interaction between bibliographers and departments, several newspaper articles, and direct communication from the dean and the collections officer to academic departments and the university community. The actual cancellations will begin early this summer.

However, what happened in parallel to this project was not typical and has served as a catalyst for a focused new strategic vision for the library–that of an electronic or digital library. As the journal cancellation project began its steady course, one faculty senator, a professor from the College of Veterinary Medicine, made a motion at the last meeting of the ISU Faculty Senate in May 1998. The motion asked that the Faculty Senate Executive Board immediately appoint a special committee to examine the issue of the journal cancellation project and work with the University Library and the University Administration to seek more effective means of addressing this difficult emergency. The motion was seconded and passed unanimously.

During the following summer, the Faculty Senate's Committee to Examine the Crisis in Scholarly Communication and Journal Subscriptions began to discuss the cancellation project and what its impact might be on the university's teaching, research, and outreach missions. What the resulting Faculty Senate Committee had to say in its final report went far beyond an examination of the journal cancellation project into an exploration of a new strategic vision for the library and what is often called the crisis in scholarly communication. The final report contains twenty-seven recommendations, recommendations that respond to the local budget crisis and recommendations that address issues facing our national academic community. The report is available on the ISU Library's home page and is referred to as the *Faculty Senate Report.*

In this paper I will provide the background to how the ISU faculty, through its Faculty Senate, became involved with pursuing a new strategic vision for the Iowa State University Library. I will then briefly describe the report and its recommendations followed by my conclusions on how the committee arrived at a much broader scope than what could have been a more traditional request to increase the overall acquisitions budget. I will conclude with a discussion on Iowa State University's next steps for implementing these recommendations and my reflections on what were the important components of the ISU process that might be of interest to other libraries involved with similar campus-wide discourses.

ESTABLISHMENT OF FACULTY SENATE COMMITTEE

As mentioned above, the ISU Faculty Senate Executive Board formed the Committee to Examine the Crisis in Scholarly Communication and Journal Subscriptions during the summer of 1998. The committee was charged to look into the state of the library's journal acquisitions budget in respect to its current cancellation project and to place the local situation in perspective with the national crisis in scholarly communication. In the early fall, at his annual convocation, the University President announced that the state of library information resources was one of three central issues facing the university for 1998/1999 and that he looked forward to receiving the Faculty Senate report. The committee was off to an auspicious start with strong leadership. The committee's membership includes seven faculty, the Dean of Library Services, the former Interim Collections Officer, the chair of the standing University Library Committee, and representatives from the Provost's Office and the President's Office. The senator who successfully brought forward the original motion chairs the committee. The purpose of this broad base membership was to bring all perspectives to bear in what would be extremely complex discussions.

The committee met biweekly from the late summer through February. Early in the process, the committee chair appointed a subcommittee to draft text and recommendations based upon committee discussions.[1] While the impetus for forming the committee was the journal cancellation project, the central issues that emerged from the committee deliberations were the changing nature of journal literature, the need to protect our core print collections, the external explosion of scholarly information resources, continuing dramatic inflation rates, and potentially dark future for wide-spread access to the academy's scholarship.

THE FACULTY SENATE REPORT

The *Faculty Senate Report* concluded that the ISU Library has lost its competitive edge in two essential and related areas. The first is infrastructure support necessary for electronic resources as part of the university's information technology strategic goal. This includes content, software and hardware.

The second is the library's acquisitions budget. The report presents a vision for building a premier electronic library and providing quality access to journal information, and it discusses mechanisms for addressing the national crisis in scholarly communication. I should note that the report does not address other components necessary for an electronic or digital library–that of services such as reference, interlibrary loan, course reserve, and instructional materials including online tutorials, gateways to Internet resources. This report only treats what I would call the traditional scholarly content commonly described as electronic literature.

The report contains twenty-seven recommendations and calls for mechanisms to measure progress towards its goals, including growth in numbers of and budget for electronic resources, comparative rank with peer institutions, stability in local collections, and participation in national initiatives related to the scholarly communication crisis. The report defines three key players (i.e., the university faculty, library, and administration) and assigns responsibilities having broad local and external implications. If the recommendations are carried forth, the resulting accomplishments will extend far beyond the current fiscal year, and well into the next century. Several of the recommendations have budget implications, others involve new ways of incorporating information needs into planning and budgeting for new academic programs and new campus initiatives. Still others involve the type of management data we must have to make informed decisions about what we purchase and decide not to purchase, and what we decide to discontinue. Finally, the report contains recommendations that could address the complex crisis facing the future of how we nationally share our scholarship.

The recommendations are broken down into three sections with corresponding goal statements.

1. Building a Nationally Recognized Electronic Library

The report's first section focuses on building a nationally recognized electronic library. By stating this goal in this manner, the concept of an electronic library is transformed into a strategic objective. While the library's Web pages already provide access to a broad array of electronic resources and services, this section provides focus to this entity and a clear mechanism to discuss its budget needs and systems support requirements. The section begins with the following practical statement:

> *The virtual bricks and mortar of the Electronic Library include both its scholarly content and its technological infrastructure. The transition to electronic information comes at a difficult time when both the physical library and the electronic library are essential to our information needs.*[2]

The committee recognized that access to library collections through electronic means is now an increasingly important benchmark in evaluating library collections as they meet learning, teaching, and research needs of students and faculty as well as the outreach functions of a land-grant institution. The committee believes that Iowa State University must be competitive nationally in the recruitment and retention of faculty as well as the recruitment, retention, graduation and career placement of its undergraduate students. An increasingly important factor in this success is and will be the university library's ability to provide electronic access to journals, books and other essential information resources and services.

The report includes two recommendations for increasing the acquisitions base budget in order to support a nationally competitive electronic library.

The first recommendation calls for a significant infusion of new acquisitions funds in support of the new "library," which now represents a vital part of the library's role in the university strategic plan's objectives for information technology (IT). While it was clear that an increase in the budget would be necessary, the primary task was to determine the methodology for deciding on the recommended amount. The committee decided to base the recommended increase on comparative data with other designated peer universities and chose to base its recommendation on the percentage all the institutions spend on electronic resources as a percentage of their total E&G. In FY1997 the highest-ranked university spent .18 percent of its total E&G expenditures on electronic resources. In order for Iowa State to reach the level of .18 percent and assuming a 6 percent inflation adjustment for FY98, FY99 and FY2000, the committee recommended an increase of $600,000 in base budget and that the library should continue its ongoing reallocation process to bring the total expenditures to a minimum of $1,110,000. This increase in funding for electronic resources would assist in:

- Catching up to our peer institutions in providing core electronic resources;
- Expanding the number of electronic resources (with or without print counterparts);
- Participating in new scholarly initiatives, such as ARL SPARC, that may help drive down the prices and/or price increases for electronic and print journals.

The second recommendation calls for reallocating internal acquisitions funds to support the electronic library. An integral part of this recommendation involves making a priority to acquire electronic-only versions of specific titles, whenever feasible. The committee had two major concerns for this particular recommendation:

- The commercial marketplace must resolve the chaotic pricing structures that now only serve to drive the costs up since frequently both print and electronic versions are required when the electronic version alone is desired;
- Publishers, librarians, and others must solve the archival issue for long-term storage of scholarly electronic materials.[3]

However, the committee believes that we cannot wait for these solutions and it remains optimistic that solutions will be found.

The committee also recommended the establishment of a technical infrastructure to ensure full access to electronic information resources to the campus community, regardless of location. This involves adequate library funding for software and hardware, and a coordinated mechanism for handling core authentication and authorization services. The core authentication and authorization services are increasingly essential due to the growing demands on remote access far beyond the library walls and traditional campus boundaries due to distance learning, students living off campus, faculty working at home or traveling, etc.

2. Quality Access to Journal Information

The second section is devoted to ensuring quality access to journal information, regardless of format, and contains twelve recommendations with the following goal:

> *University resources will never be sufficient to acquire all needed information resources to support new initiatives and programs, but a way must be found to fund our core needs and improve our purchasing capabilities to achieve and maintain a leadership position.*[4]

The recommendations include a number of suggestions to increase the base acquisitions budget in order to "soften" the journal cancellation project and continue to support legislative appropriations for inflationary increases for the acquisitions budget. In addition the report calls for:

- Adding library resource components, as appropriate, to new university academic initiatives;
- Encouraging departments and colleges to add library acquisitions components to development initiatives;
- Exploring ways that the library could expand cooperative partnerships with departments and colleges, including development of joint grant proposals and support for targeted library resources.

The report also calls for a series of recommendations that promote the most efficient use of scarce resources. These recommendations suggest that the library:

- Gather more detailed management data on the annual costs of subscriptions as well as more detailed data based on disciplines and journal usage;
- Take more advantage of potential consortial purchasing and licensing of information resources;
- Conduct a demonstration project for article-based access for a particular college, set of departments, or group of programs;
- Conduct frequent reviews to update the core and supporting journal lists for each discipline.

The call for better management data and use data emanated from faculty dissatisfaction with the concept of across-the-board percentage cancellation projects. Initially committee members found it difficult to support this methodology but soon discovered that there was little consensus on alternative approaches. Originally the University Library Committee had recommended across-the-board percentage cuts for this project because first and foremost we had no hard data to support a fair way to proceed on any other basis. The senate committee members had first assumed that differential cuts would be based upon which subject areas were inflating the highest. Of course there is a perception that the sciences are at fault; however, other disciplines, such as business, psychology, and economics, have had similar high percentage increases over recent years. Others in the university believe that the university's strengths should be supported (e.g., chemistry, physics, statistics, engineering, and computer science) to the detriment of the humanities and social sciences. Of course the humanities expenditures, even if totally cut, would hardly make a dent in the increases necessary for the sciences.

The committee decided not to make a recommendation on a future methodology but did ask the University Library Committee to take an active role advising the library on the collection and evaluation of objective data relevant to major journal cancellation projects. The report also recommends that the University Library Committee, with the university library, design a campus program of educational information on scholarly publication issues.

3. Scholarly Communication Crisis

The third section addresses the scholarly communication crisis and begins with the following statement:

> *What is at stake is the future of affordable exchange of scholarship essential to the generation of new knowledge, ideas and creative works.*[5]

This section contains the most critical set of recommendations because they involve ensuring the affordable exchange of scholarship essential to the generation of new knowledge. The committee acknowledged that solving the crisis requires fundamental change and restructuring of scholarly publishing, our notion of copyright, and our academic culture. To this end, the report includes eight recommendations that encourage local and national participation to influence change in such organizations as AAU, NASULGC, ARL's SPARC, Big 12+, NCLIS, editorial boards, and scholarly associations and societies.[6]

The report urges the Faculty Senate to encourage faculty participation in national initiatives related to the scholarly communication crisis and develop guidelines for faculty to consider in their own scholarly and professional service activities. Finally it recommends that faculty revise their department and college promotion and tenure documents taking into account the university's new local definition of scholarship, which places higher emphasis on content and influence than in the past when "numbers" were most important. The report encourages faculty to examine their heavy dependence on historical reputation of journals as an important criterion to judge the worth of colleagues' work and to emphasize the content rather than the "container."[7] The difficulty lies in the reluctance of faculty to publish in appropriate, less-costly, competing publishing venues if a major emphasis in evaluations is placed on the publisher or journal title. The result of such a change, if accompanied by an acceptable peer review, could be a reduction in the stranglehold the major commercial publishing industry has on scholarly communication.

INFLUENCES ON THE ISU PROCESS

The timing of the Iowa State University cancellation project came at the intersection of several local, regional and national events and movements, and the Faculty Senate special committee chose to view the issue of journal cancellation and the growing dependence on electronic resources in a much broader and larger context. I believe that the report provides an effective set of strategies for Iowa State University to collectively move forward in confronting the national emergencies of out-of-control inflation and publication volume. Our response is unusually comprehensive and could be seen as a blueprint for other universities. What then swayed the outcome of the committee's deliberations? I believe that it was a wide range of local and national trends and circumstances that were brought directly into committee deliberations. Timing was everything.

Of course the catalyst for this report was the cancellation project itself. Announcing a 14% across-the-board cut in the serial acquisitions budget did catch the attention of the faculty. It is quite simply what brought an influential group of faculty members around the table to begin discussing challenging issues.

The recommendations include reference to a redefinition of scholarship with a greater emphasis on content and impact through peer assessment rather than quantity and journal titles. This would not have been possible if the university had not just approved a new promotion and tenure document that includes a broadened definition of scholarship. This definition includes the scholarship of teaching, discovery, integration, and application, and it expects scholarly "output" from all faculty activities–including teaching, research, professional practice, and extension. This potential cultural shift makes way for a greater acceptance of alternative dissemination mechanisms. For example, there might be more campus support than otherwise would have been present for new electronic journals promoted through SPARC and greater interest in alternative ways to access peer-reviewed scholarship.

Iowa State University has a strong culture of strategic planning and the report's vision and recommendations interface closely with the university's strategic goals. As a result, the report exists in context of the university's strategic plan with its emphases on undergraduate education, research and graduate education, and outreach as well as leadership in information technology (IT). The recommendations associated with infrastructure support and authentication/authorization requirements relate to both the library and the campus IT infrastructure. In part under the leadership of the Information Planning Technology Group (of which the Dean of Library Services is a member) and the new Director of Academic Information Technology, a growing and renewed sense of direction and vision is emerging for information technology. The library's vision of its electronic collections and services is intricately interlaced with campus-wide IT needs.

According to the national media, the Big 12 is an athletic conference in which Iowa State University holds membership. However, the Big 12 also represents two other groups whose activities influenced committee discussions. One is the Big 12 Provosts Group, made up of the provosts at those institutions belonging to the Big 12 athletic conference. The other group is the Big 12+ Library Consortium, which includes five additional major research libraries. These two groups have been highly involved in discussing and taking action in resolving the crisis in scholarly communication.

Under the leadership of Dr. David Shulenburger, Provost at the University of Kansas, the Big 12 Provosts Group has been discussing changes to intellectual property and copyright as well as changing the nature of how we disseminate and validate the scholarship produced within our research universities. Dr. Shulenburger was an invited speaker at the fall 1998 ARL membership meeting at which he discussed his proposals for change. He began his remarks by stating that "this crisis is growing to the point that scholarship and education will be damaged significantly if we do nothing."[8] Since then he has remained an important spokesperson on this topic and has spoken at numerous state and regional forums.

A year ago, the Big 12+ Library Consortia invited members of the U.S. National Commission on Libraries and Information Science (NCLIS) to meet with library directors/deans and Provost David Shulenburger to discuss the crisis in scholarly communication. NCLIS is a permanent, independent agency of the Federal government charged by public law to advise the President and Congress on national and international library and information policies and plans. Two central concerns emerged from their discussions:

- The growing imbalance between acquisitions budgets and the volume and cost of scholarly output these libraries are expected to purchase and manage.
- Less access to scholarly communication.

Dean of Libraries James Williams II, University of Colorado at Boulder, summarized the sessions by stating, "This is the first of a series of national conversations. We ask the Commission to leverage its voice and to 'raise the volume' on conversations addressing the effective management of intellectual property in order to project and promote scholarly communication. Use the Commission's authority to hold hearings to flesh out the problems and raise the visibility, nationally and internationally, on this issue on behalf of the people that NCLIS represents–the people of the United States."[9]

NCLIS members unanimously agreed to "accept the challenge of maintaining access to significant research and scholarship at a time where both the volume and price of information have increased nearly threefold in the last decade."[10] They also established a working group to address the increasing costs of scholarly research materials in academic and research libraries. The original working group included representatives from NCLIS, the Big 12+ Consortium, the American Library Association, Information Industry Association, and the Association of Research Libraries.

The national scene has numerous other initiatives and discussions underway. For the ISU discussions the most informative discussion on the challenge of maintaining access to significant research and scholarship was the influential *Policy Perspectives: Special Issue–To Publish and Perish.*[11] This publication was derived from a roundtable of presidents, chief academic officers, librarians of major American research institutions, heads of academic publishing centers, leaders of scholarly organizations, and policy and legal experts. Many of the issues brought before NCLIS last spring arose out of the Pew roundtable discussions. The report states that "the underlying issue is the disjunction between the sociology and the economics of academic publi-

cation itself–the processes through which the research community dissemi-
nates knowledge and judges the quality of work produced by its members."[12]
The Pew report calls for regaining the initiative by:

- Ending the preoccupation with numbers;
- Being smart shoppers;
- Getting a handle on property rights;
- Investing in electronic forms of scholarly communication;
- Decoupling publication and faculty evaluation for the purposes of promotion and tenure.

The Pew report concludes by stating that "a moment of opportunity is at
hand, occasioned by the potential for peer-reviewed electronic publishing
and a sense of desperation spawned by runaway acquisitions costs. Missing
this opportunity will mean more rapidly accelerating costs, greater commercial control, and, in the end, less access to scholarly communications."[13]

Clearly the recommendations that the committee has proposed could not
have been justified without the wealth of pertinent ARL statistical data relating to the crisis in scholarly communication, the critical loss of buying power
of the largest research libraries, etc. Our discussions also benefited from the
astounding early success and national publicity surrounding ARL's SPARC
project and the national attention centered on the chilling legislative debate
on changing copyright law and fair use, particularly as it pertains to electronic resources.

WHAT ARE OUR NEXT STEPS?

While the Faculty Senate unanimously accepted the report and specifically
endorsed the budgetary recommendations, the next phases will be even more
challenging. Right now attention is focused on the library because of the
journal cancellation project, and it will be essential to keep the momentum
going and ensure that there is continued creative faculty, library and administrative leadership. The political process must continue. The committee has
taken its twenty-seven recommendations and sorted them by overall goals
and then suggested primary leadership ownership. The central points for the
faculty, college deans, and upper administration to weigh in are both financial
and cultural.

Generating continued support for what we call the electronic library remains critical. This is an essential component of the report for the library
itself as it clearly points to our future directions. While it is assumed that in
five to seven years virtually all primary research journals will be in electronic
form, there will remain disciplines whose primary scholarship will continue

to be published in monographs and whose journals are not moving as quickly as others into electronic distribution. These faculty members must be assured that this aggressive move will not jeopardize their primary information sources. Research libraries are still facing maintaining dual libraries–the physical and the digital–for both content and services.

How do we ensure that information resources are considered in the planning phases for new and changing university initiatives, new academic programs, and new faculty appointments? This recommendation will need support throughout the university and, for state-funded initiatives, through the Board of Regents. Needless to say that it will take time and perseverance to ensure success. Politically one hopes it will be recognized that these programs and initiatives will only gain in the long run from this fundamentally new planning perspective. Similarly, we need to encourage the consideration of appropriate information resources in department and college development and grant initiatives.

The report's fiscal recommendations were pivotal to the library's budget hearing and requests this spring. Other recommendations will be incorporated into library operational plans–recommendations such as the need for increased management and use data, closer consortial arrangements with the State Library of Iowa, and the Big 12+, and continued participation in SPARC. As mentioned earlier, an important part of the ongoing process will be to decide on what benchmarks will be used to determine library and campus progress. This year the campus, as well as all major units, will be revising their five-year strategic plans–I assume this report's findings will find its way into both the campus and library plans.

The report called for stronger consortial relationships among the three Iowa Regents' institutions. Since the report's publication, two meetings have been held with the respective Faculty Senate presidents, library deans, chairs of university-wide library committees, and the chief collections officers where we began discussing issues of mutual interest. The ISU Faculty Senate's report and recommendations became the focal point of our discussions. So far the most important result has been the appointment of an interinstitutional standing committee on the scholarly communication and library issues.

REFLECTIONS ON THE ISU PROCESS

What is to be drawn from the Iowa State University experience? An essential component to our success was a carefully planned integration of local, regional and national events, circumstances, and discussions. This integration led us from what would have been a useful but narrow discussion of the library's fiscal problems to an open campus dialog on the future of our library and scholarly communication. It grew out of the actions of one faculty senator, who took the initial lead, and a group of respected and dedicated faculty who were willing to spend enormous effort to build this new vision for the library. The process required a broad and influential campus forum–the senate president and its executive board chose to strongly support the process through the Faculty Senate. The committee deliberations benefited from having strong representation from the library, the Provost's Office, and the President's Office. Moreover, it was important that not only was a vision projected but that accountability was built into the recommendations. In terms of the financial recommendations, it was critical that there be a clear analytical basis for the recommendations–one that would be understandable by all campus partners. Finally, the process benefited from the close ties that the report drew from the campus culture of strategic planning and the campus's recent redefinition of scholarship within faculty evaluation processes.

In conclusion, through effective faculty leadership, this Iowa State University Faculty Senate report envisions for our campus an important new strategic future for the library. It also brings to the attention of the university faculty, the library and the administration what their potentially powerful roles might be in influencing the information marketplace. Our ultimate and collective aim should be to ensure broad and economical distribution and access to our nation's scholarship.

BIBLIOGRAPHIC REFERENCES AND NOTES

1. The Faculty Senate Committee to Examine the Crisis in Scholarly Communications and Journal Subscriptions' Drafting Subcommittee included Olivia Madison, Cynthia Dobson, David Edwards, and David Hopper (committee chair). They are the primary authors of the senate report and their contributions are reflected throughout this paper.

2. Faculty Senate Committee to Examine the Crisis in Scholarly Communication and Journal Subscriptions, *Opportunities for Pursuing a New Strategic Vision for the University Library: Report–February 3, 1999.* [Ames: Iowa State University, 1999].

3. Ibid., p. 10.

4. Ibid., p. 11.

5. Ibid., p. 16.

6. SPARC, the Scholarly Publishing & Academic Resources Coalition, is an alliance of libraries and consortiums that seek to foster expanded competition in scholarly communication. It is affiliated with the Association of Research Libraries.

7. *Faculty Senate Report*, p. 18.

8. Case, Mary M. "Provosts Propose Solutions to Journals Crisis." *ARL* 202 (February 1999), p. 1.

9. NCLIS News Release "NCLIS Accepts Challenge From the Libraries in the Heartland." 22 April 1998.

10. Ibid.

11. *To Publish and Perish*. Policy Perspectives: Special Issue, Vol. 7, and no. 4 (March 1998). Philadelphia, PA : Pew Higher Education Roundtable and the Knight Collaborative, 12 March 1998.

12. Ibid., p. 2.

13. Ibid., p. 11.

Staffing for Collection Development in the Electronic Environment: Toward a New Definition of Roles and Responsibilities

Deborah Jakubs

INTRODUCTION

Like most jobs in research libraries, the position of collection development librarian–bibliographer, resource specialist, subject specialist, whichever term is used–has undergone a dramatic change in the past two decades. Once almost exclusively focused on materials selection, the responsibilities of the librarian engaged in collection development now extend to the creation and maintenance of Web sites, intensive faculty outreach, teaching, specialized reference service, fund-raising, and other tasks. And yet, although the nature of the work we call "collection development" has changed, the image of the bibliographer and of the complexity of his or her work has generally not. This is due in large part to the continued compartmentalization of library work, at least in our minds, and to the persistence of traditional organizational categories. Our structures have not kept pace with our functions.

Even when libraries have been restructured and divisions have been given new names, the work is still perceived as belonging either to technical services, public services, or collection development. In fact, collection development is hybrid work, incorporating both technical and public service. Positions that blur the lines among these organizational units are difficult to define and to evaluate.

Deborah Jakubs is Director, Collections Service, Duke University.

[Haworth co-indexing entry note]: "Staffing for Collection Development in the Electronic Environment: Toward a New Definition of Roles and Responsibilities." Jakubs, Deborah. Co-published simultaneously in *Journal of Library Administration* (The Haworth Information Press, an imprint of The Haworth Press, Inc.) Vol. 28, No. 4, 1999, pp. 71-83; and: *Collection Development in the Electronic Environment: Shifting Priorities* (ed: Sul H. Lee) The Haworth Information Press, an imprint of The Haworth Press, Inc., 1999, pp. 71-83. Single or multiple copies of this article are available for a fee from The Haworth Document Delivery Service [1-800-342-9678, 9:00 a.m. - 5:00 p.m. (EST). E-mail address: getinfo@haworthpressinc.com].

In this article, I would like to discuss the image and reality of what we call "collection development" work, examine new definitions and job descriptions, and suggest ideas for training and mentoring, as well as models for developing expectations and mechanisms for evaluating the work of the collection development librarian. My perceptions derive from my own experience in a variety of spheres–as bibliographer, as department head, as a Title VI area studies center director and adjunct faculty member in History, and as Director of Collections Services. Of course many different models exist for "doing collection development," because of the many ways that libraries have adapted their collection development structures over the years, and no one model will suit every situation. Elements from different models can be combined and utilized in various settings, depending on the staffing patterns and the local needs.

"BIBLIOGRAPHERS ARE A LUXURY"

At a 1995 conference on "The Future of Area Librarians," I was invited to make a presentation on the conference theme, focusing on the image of the area librarian. Many of my comments then are relevant to today's broader focus on the collection development librarian.

During the 1960s and 1970s, when the idea of hiring subject specialists in academic libraries in response to the growth of area studies programs within universities was still new, the topic generated a modest body of literature. As attention turned in the 1980s toward more general collection management issues, writing on subject librarians has dwindled. There are a few potentially relevant articles here and there, which fall neatly into several groups, covering the standard topics: the full-time/part-time bibliographer dilemma; the question of credentials, i.e., whether bibliographers need a second master's degree or a PhD; academic status and publishing or perishing among librarians; self-image and leadership qualities. One as-yet unpublished article, co-authored by Mark Grover, Susan Fales, and Larry Ostler, entitled "Reference and Collection Development: Are They Compatible?" addresses head-on yet another of "the issues" for bibliographers, namely, whether or not collection development and reference work blend naturally and should be combined in the same positions.[1] The article also analyzes the personality differences between bibliographers and reference librarians. There is an excellent 1994 article by Allen Veaner, entitled, "Paradigm Lost, Paradigm Regained? A Persistent Personnel Issue in Academic Librarianship, II," in which the author contends, among many other things, that librarians' intellectual and programmatic responsibilities are undelegatable and, hence, that subject specialists are indispensable.[2] This is a rather different view from that expressed in 1978 at a meeting of the Association of College and Research Libraries

(ACRL) by Dennis Dickenson, who presented a paper entitled, "Subject Specialists in Academic Libraries: The Once and Future Dinosaurs."[3] He claimed that the economic conditions in research libraries have "rendered obsolete" many of the original justifications for the subject specialist: "It may very well be that that insofar as they require, in order to be effective, very substantial book funds on which to draw, and their relatively high salaries come from money which could otherwise be used directly for acquisitions, restoration, preservation, etc."

Dickenson's view of the role of subject specialists in libraries is narrow; he sees limits to their potential contributions to the organization. That is not an accurate view any longer, if it ever was, as recent developments in the work of collection development librarians have demonstrated. I contend that subject librarians are more necessary than ever before, and that the definition of what constitutes "collection development work" must be expanded.

WHAT IS COLLECTION DEVELOPMENT?

The whole concept of what constitutes "collection development" has changed, and perhaps we should look there for a new definition of the role of the bibliographer. We have moved from a time of ample resources (at least looking back from today's vantage point they seem to have been ample) to a time of largely static budgets, with many more demands on those funds. This has shifted the focus of collection development from local collection-building to more cooperative ventures, and toward a heavier reliance on resource sharing.

In the interest of efficiency, there has been a move toward more use of approval plans as a means of acquiring current publications. While this has changed the job of the selector, it will not eliminate it. In fact, most approval plans require a great deal of monitoring, from the initial profile design to the regular review of materials. This is especially true with non-English language approval plans. Approval plans have many advantages, particularly the speed with which they bring new publications to the library, without going through the order process. But they can also be partially responsible for an alarming recent trend, namely, that collections, particularly in some fields, are coming to resemble each other more and more. Approval plans alone cannot provide all the books needed in a research library; they must be carefully supplemented by firm-orders by librarians knowledgeable about the collections and the curricula. We cannot outsource collection development decisions to approval plan providers.

Reduced acquisitions because of net decreases in funding have also required more careful selection of materials. After all, it is easier to spend a large budget than a small one. This has added to the job of the collection development librarian, as has the need in recent years to conduct large-scale serials cancellations, not a frequent occurrence in collection development programs in the 1970s. Redirecting a very significant portion of the serials budget toward electronic access paid on an annual basis is another trend in libraries, and has had, even while bringing exciting and powerful new resources to campus, a negative effect on collecting in support of disciplines that are more monograph-dependent. It has also, as we know, reduced the flexibility in our materials budgets as a higher percentage of our funding is directed each year toward ongoing commitments.

Many of these changes are explored in a recent unpublished paper by Joseph Branin, Frances Groen, and Suzanne Thorin, entitled, "The Changing Nature of Collection Management in Research Libraries."[4] The authors examine the contemporary history of collection management and particularly the new environment that is the result of the information technology transition. This has led to the coexistence of two information systems, one print and one digital. "In some libraries, collection development staff came late to digital resources, and as a result they let other parts of the organization–administration, systems, or reference–take on the responsibility for selection decisions regarding electronic databases."[5] They discuss "new boundaries and new structures for collection development," highlighting the acquisition of reference tools, electronic journals, and digital archives of historical materials in bundled packages. The authors point out that collection boundaries are changing, and ask "What is a local collection in a networked environment?" The virtual communities of libraries that have emerged offer new opportunities for cooperative collection development. All of these changes have powerful implications for the work of the collection development librarian.

But collection development work does not stop at these acquisitions functions. It includes as well the follow-up to the selection decisions, publicizing the collections, assisting patrons in their use, and expanding access to resources that may not even be held locally. The collection development librarian, as discussed below, now has a range of functions that extends well beyond what has generally been considered part of the job.

THE IMAGE AND THE PARADOX

The bibliographer does not enjoy a positive image in all circles, partly because the job was formerly highly independent and rather narrowly conceived. In order to implement a new system that makes the best use of subject specialists, we must reject the stereotypes, and use a different term to describe the role, although I have not yet come up with a term that satisfies me entirely. One important reason for the sometimes negative image is that the work of the collection development librarian is not widely understood, or easily quantifiable in these days of justifying FTEs based on their productivity. The terms that come to some minds within libraries, in connection with bibliographers, are far from complimentary: "elitist," "arrogant," "print-bound," "faculty wanna-be," "idiosyncratic," "privileged," "prima donna," "traditional." "What do they do all day?" "Can't we put them on the reference desk?" And yet this view is unfair, outdated, and destructive. It is, ironically, precisely the successful fulfillment of the collection development librarian's job–the rapport with faculty, the close association with and dedication to academic programs, part and parcel of the job, the broad subject knowledge and an intensity of engagement with the field–that create the paradox. Doing these things well both allows the librarian to support the mission of the institution, to satisfy faculty and students, enjoying personal satisfaction and intellectual stimulation in the process, and yet also provokes the development or the perpetuation of a negative image. Why this paradox? And why is collection development work so poorly understood?

I believe it is because bibliographers and their image carry a great deal of baggage. The image problem can be a two-way street. Some may warrant the uncomplimentary terms used above, behaving in ways that betray their own insecurities. Some may not want an expanded role, or may resist the changes in their job descriptions and expectations. And yet those who do will be left behind, if they have not already been, as the job has expanded from largely solitary work to a much more complex set of responsibilities. In my presentation at the Indiana conference, this was the theme: that the future of area librarians (and of subject specialists in general) depends on adapting and modernizing, integrating their skills into the library in new ways, thereby changing their image. At the core of this is a fact that we sometimes neglect to acknowledge: that all librarians are critical resources, partners with faculty. We need faculty and they need us. We do not want to be them; we want to facilitate their work, and that of their students. We want to build deep, coherent collections, and to see them used. The better our relationships with faculty, the better our position to explain processes and changes in the library and to solicit their input on a wide variety of library issues that may affect them. In other words, collection development librarians with regular contact with faculty can serve as a conduit for information traveling in both directions. The bibliographer, regardless of number or type of advanced degrees, can play a wide variety of roles within the university and thus achieve a certain visibility that enhances the image of the library. I have concluded that it is the personal contacts that people have with librarians that cause them to form opinions about the library. Thus, an expanded role for those with collection development responsibilities is an important goal.

TOWARD A NEW DEFINITION

Changes in the job responsibilities and functions of collection development librarians have occurred relatively gradually in most libraries but not yet in people's minds. Collection development duties may have been assigned on top of another position, with no clearly written job description. To codify these adaptations, and to recognize the new constellation of job responsibilities, we need to examine the larger organizational structure in which collection development takes place. There is still a tendency to isolate what are considered the collection development aspects of the job–which will vary by institution, but generally focus on materials selection–from any other activities, and classify people as "full-time" or "part-time" bibliographers.

What are the implications of this distinction? What does the "full-time" person do that the "part-time " collection development librarian doesn't do? The answer should be "nothing," with the result that we erase the distinction between the two pseudo-quantitative measures of time spent on collection development, and develop a standard set of duties that will be carried out regardless of the areas of responsibility. The tasks that make up the job of the collection development librarian under a new definition, or perhaps a definition that more accurately reflects the reality of work in libraries, include everything ranging from selection of materials in multiple formats (the most obvious task) to creating online user guides, with many things in between. If we view resource selection as the very first step on the continuum of public service, and bibliographers as primarily responsible for that step, it makes sense for them to continue to play a public function (while attending to questions that may emerge from the technical sphere, related to location, language, availability of materials, assignment of vendor, preservation, etc.) moving along the continuum. Into the mix fall many other responsibilities, all related to the area or discipline on which the librarian focuses: the review of gifts and decisions on whether they should be added to the collections; monitoring exchange relationships, when relevant; developing a thorough knowledge of the electronic resources that support the field; assisting patrons in their use; providing specialized research assistance; playing an expanded role in fund-raising for the library, by initiating and/or contributing to grant proposals and working with library development staff; developing relationships with publishers; teaching courses, as relevant in his/her fields, from a combined bibliographic/disciplinary perspective, and/or team-teaching one or more sessions with faculty. Publicizing the library's collections, maintaining a Web page with links to many other resources, and pursuing an energetic outreach effort to faculty and students are additional responsibilities of the collection development librarian. There is no reason for them to function behind the scenes.

In recent years, many libraries have hired "electronic access librarians."

This reflects an assumption that the format takes precedence over the content of a database or Internet resource. This is consistent with the observation in the paper by Branin, Thorin and Groen that collection development librarians have often ceded responsibility for selecting electronic resources to systems, administrative, or reference staff. I believe that all librarians who are responsible for selecting materials should cover all formats, consulting as necessary with reference and systems regarding ease of use, compatibility issues, etc. They should be conversant with the features of any databases of interest to their users, and able to interpret and publicize those sources. They are also responsible for creating access, through the Web, to other resources that may be remote but also relevant. Therefore, all collection development librarians, who assist users in discovering the potential of the resources available to them, should also be "electronic access librarians." It is a critical part of their jobs.

The increased focus on cooperation and collaboration in libraries has been mentioned, and new formats have brought with them new opportunities to design cooperative projects. The intellectual oversight of such projects should fall to the collection development librarian, whether the range of the cooperation is local–on one's own campus–or regional, national, or international. The kinds of projects that the Global Resources Program, jointly sponsored by the Association of American Universities and the Association of Research Libraries (AAU/ARL), is implementing, for example, require the very active participation of dozens of collection development librarians, as well as interlibrary loan and document delivery staff.[6] These and other projects, whose goal is to expand access to scholarly resources within a constrained budgetary environment through the use of new technologies and a new interdependence among libraries, require extremely careful design, budgeting, and truly collegial implementation for their success. It has been said that the longest lasting and best functioning cooperative collection development agreements are those that are hammered out among the people who know the collections best, the bibliographers. They cannot be legislated from above. I foresee much time and energy on the part of collection development librarians in future years going into such endeavors not only for the benefit of local users but in the interest of the collectivity as well.

In order to carry out this expanded set of tasks, the collection development librarian needs time. In conversations with a wide variety of resource specialists, this is the message that I have consistently heard: that the job has many more facets than ever before, and that this change should be acknowledged in the job description.

WHO OWNS PUBLIC SERVICE?

Collection development librarians, if they are doing their jobs, have a very visible and significant public service role. This is not always acknowledged, because "public service" has come to be associated primarily with general reference work. This has led to the creation of composite positions in which reference librarians also "do" collection development, but their reference work is generally more urgent, leaving selection duties for later, quieter moments. Frequently, their collection development work is not covered in their annual evaluations, except in a cursory manner. These are the people who feel especially acutely the lack of time to carry out their duties adequately. At times of fiscal stringency, i.e., most of the time these days in libraries, one means of saving money is to combine positions, or combine into one position tasks formerly done by two people. One of the most common means of consolidation of function has been to move collection development librarians into reference, and to assign them hours on the reference desk, or to assign to reference librarians collection development responsibilities. I believe that this seriously misinterprets the work of both groups of librarians, and that this "merger" is not in the best interest of either group. At best it only grafts a set of collection development responsibilities onto a general reference position, and leaves the librarian with a sense of having two sometimes competing jobs–one as a specialist, and one as a generalist–and not enough time to do either of them well.

This may be exacerbated by the fact that a librarian's own professional self-image does not integrate the roles, so, for example, someone considers herself "a reference librarian who also does collection development for history." Another person is "a bibliographer who works eight hours in reference." Naturally the questions that I am raising here also pertain to the field of general reference and how it is best carried out, and by whom. I know from experience that it can be disastrous to put the wrong people in reference, just as it can lead to negative results to assume that anyone can "do" collection development. How do we achieve a new model in which the special knowledge and skills of the collection development librarians are put to the very best use, and their public service role is acknowledged, beyond general reference?

A SET OF SKILLS, AND WAYS TO DEVELOP THEM

Harold Billings, Director of Libraries at the University of Texas at Austin, commented recently that we make a mistake in libraries when we look too narrowly to fill positions. He elaborated, pointing out that successful sports teams do not always seek the very best point guard, or right wing, or half-back. They look for the very best athletes, with a set of skills that will serve them well in a variety of positions. Of course, in collection development, there are certain skills (knowledge of a subject, language ability, etc.) that must be prerequisites. But more and more, since the range of activities of a subject specialist is so broad, adaptability and a broad view of the work of the library may be almost equally important.

What skills should a collection development librarian have, in addition to a strong subject background and an interest in the job? A preliminary list would include: an engagement with issues for research libraries on the national level, e.g., copyright and other scholarly communication issues; a basic understanding of the internal functioning of the library, and the interrelationships among departments; how the collections budget is allocated and managed; strong interpersonal skills; a basic understanding of technical services; a familiarity with publishing and the book trade; and very strong writing skills. Teaching ability, called upon in user education, is another important attribute, as is a thorough understanding of all of the tools available for assisting users with a particular research need. As users spend more time on the Web, the ability to conceptualize and develop a dynamic Web presence for a particular subject is becoming critical as well. If we consider that "collection development" now extends way beyond what a bibliographer might amass in a single institution, to distant resources held elsewhere or even virtually, building links to those resources becomes a fundamental job for the collection development librarian.

All of these changes have happened quickly, and adapting to them is not always easy or comfortable. We should provide collection development librarians with opportunities for continuing education whenever possible. This can be arranged locally, through job exchanges, cross-training, or team-teaching, or through participation in more formal workshops and conferences.

Do collection development librarians need an MLS to be effective? This could be the topic of another paper, or even of another conference. I have discovered that it is an emotionally charged issue that does not always lend itself to calm discussion. Let me just describe one example of a new approach to training bibliographers, and the thinking that went into its development.

Following the 1995 Indiana conference, where a primary concern had been the future of area librarians, The Andrew W. Mellon Foundation expressed interest in entertaining a proposal for a new training program for such specialists, specifically those focused on Latin America. Duke University Libraries received a multi-year grant in support of a post-doctoral program that would bring a recent PhD recipient in any field of Latin American studies to campus for a year to become immersed in the workings of the library and provide them with a thorough training program. This would give these post-doctoral fellows the practical and detailed library experience to complement their already strong subject knowledge. The program is still functioning, and the two individuals who have completed the post-doc are gainfully employed as librarians. They consider themselves to be librarians, despite the lack of an MLS degree, and are enjoying their work enormously. I have many colleagues in the libraries at Duke to thank for their role in preparing the fellows for their new careers.

Based partly on the apparent success of the Duke program, the Mellon Foundation made another award to Indiana University for a similar program to train African Studies and Slavic Studies librarians. This is a more recent program, but every indication is that its "graduates" will also be extremely well-prepared to work in the field. In both programs, Duke's and Indiana's, the fellows are encouraged to audit a limited number of library school courses, but are not required or expected to pursue the formal degree. Both programs assume that to be a successful collection development librarian one needs a strong subject/language background along with a solid basic understanding of the functioning of the modern research library. It has been suggested that a similar internship program, not necessarily limited to applicants with the PhD, might be a useful approach to train science librarians, also in relatively short supply.

EVALUATION

It is widely believed that one of the most difficult personnel evaluations to carry out is the assessment of the bibliographer. "How can I know if she or he is selecting the right books and journals?" says the AUL. "I don't know the languages and I am not a specialist in that subject." While it is true that a micro-evaluation of materials selection for each bibliographer is well beyond the realm of possibility for an administrator, I believe that collection development librarians, if they are fulfilling all the roles described above, are easily evaluated through a combination of approaches: observing relationships with other librarians; requesting feedback from peers; soliciting opinions from faculty, not necessarily specifically on "the person" of the librarian, but on the state of the collection, the means and frequency of communication, and the level of service provided. Does she have wide engagement in the field, competency in teaching and in explaining the use of different resources? Is he visible and accessible to his users? Has he created a well-designed Web page for the subjects and/or areas under his stewardship, including a link to a clear description of the collection strengths and to collecting policies? Does that page include a branching out to resources of relevance to the subject but not necessarily locally held? And last but certainly not least, how is her budget management? Does she monitor spending well? Over- or under-spend? All of these are ways, though not an exhaustive list, to determine the effectiveness of the collection development librarian. It is also important for each librarian to identify a set of goals for the year ahead.

NEW MODELS

Well-prepared, knowledgeable, and responsive collection development people who perform a variety of tasks are among the best resources the library has. Through them, faculty and students have a contact who not only anticipates needs for materials but also serves as an information point and a source of specialized research assistance. This follow-through with the public is really the core function for the new collection development librarian. It approaches the staffing issue from the user's perspective, providing a versatile resource person for all areas, someone who spends collections money wisely because of having developed a broad perspective on the needs of his or her constituency and the university community.

We should turn the needs of our patrons to our advantage and equip ourselves with the knowledge to satisfy their demands. The process of educating faculty must be conducted one-on-one. Few faculty members are interested in attending meetings to learn about the library functions. They are primarily interested in what can help them specifically, in learning what they need to know to take the next step in their research, to get books ordered for reserves, etc. It is our job to understand and anticipate patrons' needs and to display our knowledge and ability as part of our job. Faculty respond well to librarians they respect and trust to interpret their needs, and news travels fast within academic departments. Patrons, especially faculty, can be both our worst detractors and our most loyal and vocal supporters. In the chain of educating the university community about the library and librarians, this kind of direct communication with faculty, whether it involves consulting on the value of adding a periodical title to the collection or discussing the features of a new database, is the strongest link.

One further point on image: the library and the librarian are more constant than the faculty in the life of the university. Librarians teach useful skills. In many cases, students learn from librarians skills on which they will rely throughout their lives. Thus, the librarian can play a critical role in the university and should be encouraged to pursue broader involvement. This may include participating in university-wide committees, not only those with direct relevance for the library. Curriculum committees, for example, or program review committees, can benefit from the perspective of the specialist librarian. We are in an excellent position to learn daily about the educational process at our respective institutions through formal and informal relationships. We must take the initiative to make worthwhile contributions of our ideas and energy to the university.

I have spent considerable time thinking about new structures to enable the collection development functions described in this paper to be institutionalized within the library, to make collections the focus of our work. I have not yet devised the perfect model for Duke, but I am convinced that it needs to undo, somehow, our traditional work categories. It is not as simple as merging everyone into a single very large department and making them responsible for a wide array of duties. The goal is to create a fluid environment in which departmental lines may still be important for administrative purposes but in which individuals with distinctive capabilities and knowledge bases work together to build collections, assist users at all levels, and design the future of library services.

CONCLUSION

I was fortunate, during February, to spend two weeks at Koc University in Istanbul, Turkey, as part of an exchange that Duke has with this relatively new, English-language university. I was consulting on collection development, and evaluating the library's support for a certificate program in American Studies. I formed close relationships with the staff and was deeply moved by their commitment to serving the students and faculty at Koc, and to developing their skills as much as possible. In Turkish universities, collection development has generally been the responsibility of the faculty, although it is widely acknowledged by faculty and librarians alike (as well as by university administrators) that this is not the ideal situation. Those of us who are familiar with the pros and cons of relying on faculty for balanced selection of materials will understand why. In any case, one of the points I made to the Koc University provost, with the full support of the faculty, was that he should consider a new system in which librarians who have an academic background adequate to do selection are formally given that responsibility (most of the books ordered each year are ordered not by faculty but by librarians already). On my last day in Istanbul, I made a presentation on collection development to librarians from various institutions in the city, and it was a fine preparation for this paper. I spoke of the importance of integrating roles within the library, of having a transparent process for faculty, in which librarians, by virtue of working closely with them as partners, anticipate needs, seek frequent feedback, and build collections accordingly. These same librarians work with students in classes to reinforce their knowledge of curricular concerns, and provide to the students a dynamic library instruction program that introduces them to many different types of sources. To move from the present situation at Koc and other Turkish university libraries to one that more closely resembles ours will be a big step, but the situations are really quite similar, and I was struck by the universality of certain issues: the library has the chance to prove its central role, and the librarian the opportunity to forge direct, collegial relationships with faculty, administrators, and other patrons, educating them to the problems and potential of the library. It requires a high level of confidence in our role, both real and potential, and an organizational vision that goes beyond traditional categories to a new, adaptable structure that encourages a strong intellectual commitment and an innovative approach to service.

NOTES

1. Fales, Susan, Mark Grover, and Larry Ostler. "Reference and Collection Development: Are They Compatible?" Unpublished manuscript, Harold B. Lee Library, Brigham Young University, June 1993.

2. Veaner, Allen. "Paradigm Lost, Paradigm Regained? A Persistent Personnel Issue in Academic Librarianship, II." *College and Research Libraries*, September 1994, pp. 389-402.

3. Dickenson, Dennis W. "Subject Specialists in Academic Libraries: The Once and Future Dinosaurs." In *New Horizons for Academic Libraries*, National Conference of the Association of College and Research Libraries (1st: 1978: Boston). Edited by Robert D. Stueart. Munich and London: Saur, 1979, pp. 438-444.

4. Groen, Frances, Suzanne Thorin, and Joesph Branin. "The Changing Nature of Collection Management in Research Libraries: Points for Discussion." Prepared for the Research Collections Committee of the Association of Research Libraries, October 1998.

5. Ibid., p. 3.

6. See the AAU/ARL Global Resources Program website: http://www.arl.org/collect/grp/

Consortia and Collections:
Achieving a Balance Between Local Action and Collaborative Interest

Barbara McFadden Allen

Today's collection manager faces unprecedented challenge and opportunity in meeting the needs of library users. A number of factors are forcing sometimes radical shifts in collections budgets and strategies, while the emergence of truly effective network technology offers opportunity for substantive cooperative collection management. Why should collection managers embrace collaboration as a tool for effective management of collections? And how are local needs balanced against the collective needs of a consortium or other cooperative group? The answers to these questions might best be found by first reviewing the factors that are forcing change. These factors include:

- Changes in societal attitudes towards higher education;
- Increasing budget and service pressures;
- Copyright, licensing, and intellectual property issues;
- Preservation and the creation of permanent archives of information;
- All of these leading to changes in collection building.

A quick review of each of these areas gives shape and direction to the questions about how to deal effectively with these changes.

CHANGES IN SOCIETAL ATTITUDES TOWARDS HIGHER EDUCATION

Changes in societal attitudes towards higher education in general will dramatically affect our libraries. The politics of survival will come into play

Barbara McFadden Allen is Director, CIC Center for Library Initiatives and Assistant Director of the Committee on Institutional Cooperation.

[Haworth co-indexing entry note]: "Consortia and Collections: Achieving a Balance Between Local Action and Collaborative Interest." Allen, Barbara McFadden. Co-published simultaneously in *Journal of Library Administration* (The Haworth Information Press, an imprint of The Haworth Press, Inc.) Vol. 28, No. 4, 1999, pp. 85-90; and: *Collection Development in the Electronic Environment: Shifting Priorities* (ed: Sul H. Lee) The Haworth Information Press, an imprint of The Haworth Press, Inc., 1999, pp. 85-90. Single or multiple copies of this article are available for a fee from The Haworth Document Delivery Service [1-800-342-9678, 9:00 a.m. - 5:00 p.m. (EST). E-mail address: getinfo@haworthpressinc.com].

as university administrators react to the demands of a public calling for increased financial accountability from our universities; for affordable undergraduate education; and for increased focus on undergraduate teaching and learning. This, in turn, will affect university and library administration in both positive and negative ways. In the new economic environment, universities and colleges will perhaps be more selective about programs offered, resulting in greater specialization. The growth of electronic communities of scholars will affect the academy in ways we cannot even predict, but certainly, fulfilling the information needs of "virtual patrons" will challenge us. And, as universities embrace distance learning and reach out to communities beyond the campus–essentially delivering a curriculum electronically–how does the library provide concomitant access to and delivery of curriculum support to the remote users?

While such economic, social, and political pressures are brought to bear on the academy, our accrediting systems–for both libraries and academic programs–have not responded to such changes. Old models of evaluation are certainly evident in the evaluation of libraries, where we are to this day engaged in "bigger is better" evaluation–in spite of the fact that we are increasingly dependent upon *access* to materials as opposed to *ownership* of materials.

INCREASING BUDGET AND SERVICE PRESSURES

In a situation by no means unique to higher education or the academic and research library, we face increasing budget pressures that will require completely new service models and budget strategies. Elimination of duplication of effort, consolidation of services and departments, and general downsizing of staff will increase as economic pressures and constraints are put upon us. This may create significant changes in what an academic library professional is (or does). I've heard it said that we will have to shift funds from processes to services, and this makes such eminently good sense that it bears repeating–we will have to shift funds from processes to services.

These pressures rise from a variety of sources: the need to invest (and continually re-invest) in a network infrastructure capable of meeting demand for the delivery of digital information and the fact that our acquisitions budgets cannot keep pace with either the rate of publication or the rate of inflation are perhaps the greatest factors influencing budgets. Eli Noam offers a powerful example of the explosive growth of publishing in the sciences. Most branches of science, Noam reports, show an exponential growth of about 4-8% annually, with a doubling period of 10 to 15 years. As an illustration of this trend, Chemical Abstracts took 31 years (1907 to 1937) to publish its first 1 million abstracts; the second million took 18 years; the most recent million took only 1.75 years. Thus, more articles on chemistry were published between 1993 and 1995 than throughout history before 1900.[1]

COPYRIGHT, LICENSING, AND INTELLECTUAL PROPERTY ISSUES

Here lies a complicated web of issues, challenges, and concerns. Proposed revisions of copyright law seem to be written in response to the needs and interests of the entertainment industry rather than the "intellectual or scholarly" industry. Many publishers suggest that greater restrictions should be placed on electronic resources; that there should be no such thing as "fair use" within the electronic environment; and that digital information should be made available on a "cost per use" model. In such an environment, what happens to the "free" flow of information so necessary to support knowledge systems and stimulate intellectual discussion? How can a library support the use of a system in which they pay for information each time an information "packet" (i.e., electronic article) is used? And, if the costs must be borne by the users, what happens to the free flow of information in unpopular or traditionally underfunded disciplines? To say nothing of the potential impact of "pay as you go" pricing models on publishers who have relied upon the predictable revenue streams generated by the "just in case" purchasing model supported by many research libraries.

While debate on copyright revision continues, some vendors offer licenses for electronic resources which are dramatically restrictive–suggesting, for instance, that any retention of the objects in digital format is prohibited–that, for instance, a researcher may not download an article for ready reference, but may only view the item as a "transient file." At the same time, within the academic community, there is a growing enthusiasm for the notion that faculty authors might grant liberal use rights to the universities in which they work.

PRESERVATION AND THE CREATION OF PERMANENT ARCHIVES OF INFORMATION

The research library has traditionally accepted the role of steward to a large body of printed materials. This stewardship, by definition, includes the retention of all materials acquired, and such retention necessarily includes the conservation and preservation of these materials in order to meet the needs of the scholarly research community. No doubt you are familiar with the race to preserve materials printed on paper that is literally self-destructing. And, even as librarians seek ways to protect and preserve these increasingly delicate collections, librarians are under great pressure to use their scarce resources for networked information resources. If faced with the choice of spending $100,000 on deacidification of brittle books, or installing new public access terminals, you can guess which path will likely be taken.

Too, librarians are only now struggling with methods of preserving digital information–and ensuring that the information will be useful in the future. Methods of keeping a dynamic digital file of information–such as refreshing or migrating the data–will be necessary, but where are the blueprints for such a system?

CHANGES IN COLLECTION BUILDING

All of the challenges and conditions I've discussed will affect the way we build collections. The issues and trends associated with collection building, collection management, and access to and delivery of information fall within the rubric of the great challenge we face in providing consistent, coherent access to a body of knowledge of sufficient depth and breadth to support both undergraduate learning and graduate, post-graduate, and research needs. Traditionally, of course, this challenge has been met by libraries working in a fairly isolated environment. The librarian selected materials from an available universe of published materials, making that material available within the physical confines of the library. How do we translate this important skill to the digital environment? Too, in the past, the user was generally unaware of the range of other possibilities available–an oversimplification and generalization, to be sure–but the user could not have daily interaction, for instance, with the catalogs of thousands of libraries as is currently possible on the Internet. The great past challenge, then, was reconciling the gap between what the library could purchase and what was available for purchase. Our great present challenge is the gap between what can be made available to users locally, and what they know to be available elsewhere. The choice of the term "what can be made available to users locally" is a deliberate one: a user might see that literally hundreds of resources are available within their area of expertise at another university, but no provision has been made to access such materials locally through traditional interlibrary loan or digital delivery systems, or through creative licensing arrangements.

Furthermore, we've traditionally organized physical objects (through classification for instance)–but how do we translate that organizing quality to the electronic environment? Certainly, this challenge is not unique to academic libraries, but the problem is exacerbated by the research library model of the past; acquiring all materials, in all formats, within a given discipline becomes increasingly complicated and expensive–as the publication rate–in formats both digital and traditional–increases.

As we strive to develop collaborative programs, we must remain flexible in application. That is, the environment is changing so rapidly that those solutions we identify today may not be the solutions we need for tomorrow. We need to constantly evaluate our activities and actions. I'm particularly struck by the rather labor-intensive methodologies we've put in place to support collaborative acquisitions. Successful cooperative collection building must, I think, be defined broadly. We must set up a decision-making infrastructure that supports collaborative decision making at every step of the way. This implies broad descriptions of collections and their relative "depth"–a conspectus of some sort, as well as title-level descriptions including on-order information. The subject level information can help the collection manager make budget decisions–if we have to cut $20,000 where can we cut it and know that we will still have access to this information–where to invest in document delivery–and where collections must be "protected."

At the subject specialist and order level, the title level information will guide decision making on a day-to-day basis as decisions are made about purchasing individual titles–especially helpful when purchasing expensive sets of information. I believe that pilot acquisitions programs build a sound foundation of human networks, but taking the next step towards insuring that interdependence and reliability upon one another is as natural as working with your own departmental libraries is a large step. Having said all of that, there is certainly no reason to expect the process of cooperative collection management and/or cooperative acquisitions of digital resources will be less complicated than the structures we have in place for acquiring and managing collections.

RESPONSIVE ACTION TO THESE CHALLENGES

I think the byword for responsive reaction to these challenges is collaboration. At the university level, administrators, faculty, and researchers must be perceived as vital partners to their respective citizens, legislators, and communities. The public supports that which they feel directly affects them and their families. If the university is collaborating with industry and community to provide distance learning for the citizens; if the university is collaborating with government to find ways to apply research to improve the lives of the citizens; if the university is collaborating with schools to ensure that all K-12 students have the potential to attend college–then, the university can not only sway public opinion, it will be seen as important an infrastructure element as the highway system or telecommunications systems.

If libraries collaborate with one another, the user may realize dramatic improvements in access to information. Within the CIC, 12 major teaching and research universities have embraced the concept that they share one large information resource. Thus, when the vision becomes a reality, the students, faculty and staff of our universities will have access to a collection of some 60 million book volumes and countless digital and electronic resources. Creative budgeting strategies in this environment allow individual libraries to concentrate purchases in areas specific to the research "flavor" of their universities while foregoing areas outside their academic "scope." Acquisitions monies might be used for any acquisition–whether permanent (purchasing) or discreet (borrowing). Licenses can be drawn up for access by the entire population–in this case half a million students across 12 universities–rather than on a case-by-case basis. Further, librarians can collaborate with campus computing and university administration to identify new budget strategies and models for providing ubiquitous access to networked information and for the design and implementation of archives for digital information.

Librarians, researchers, and publishers can form "collaboratories" to experiment with new publishing models designed for the digital environment. Working together, these partners can address the need for librarians to have predictable and reasonable costs for information, satisfy the publisher's needs for predictable, appropriate levels of revenue, and protect the interests of the writers and researchers.

Working together and reaching out to appropriate and willing partners not only strengthens us, but gives us competitive advantage.

There are many challenges, issues, and trends that I don't have time to address today (perhaps much to your relief), but I want to encourage each of you to accept a personal challenge to develop the personal skills you will need in the collaborative environment of the future. Flexibility, enthusiasm, inquisitiveness, and the willingness to accept and adapt to rapid change will be essential skills. Many people say libraries are going through an evolutionary period. That implies, I think, a rather leisurely shift and change over many years. The truth is that we are undergoing a metamorphosis.

NOTE

1. Eli M. Noam, "Electronics and the Dim Future of the University," Science 270 (Oct. 1995): 247-49.

Setting Journal Priorities
by Listening to Customers

Karen Hunter

Scholarly journals have been around since 1665. I have been involved in buying and selling them for 32 years, about 10% of the total time journals have existed. In those 32 years with which I am familiar, scientific journals moved from the very heady days of their second phase (the extraordinary post-World War II burst of growth, fed by greatly expanding international research, proliferating university campuses, and voracious library collection developers) into the just-launched and uncertain third phase, marked by tight budgets, the Web and a reexamination of the roles played by all participants.[1,2] While perhaps not as extreme as a rollercoaster, the ride has certainly had its ups and downs and there were times when we all had an uneasy feeling in our stomachs.

Doing strategic planning during such a tumultuous period is difficult. It is essential to set priorities and stay focused. In business school you are taught that the objective of the enterprise is to get and retain customers. This means understanding and meeting customer needs.

Journal publishing, whether for profit or not, has this as its objective as well. And for most journal publishers there are at least four sets of customers: (1) authors and editors; (2) purchasers; (3) readers; and (4) owners. There are overlaps among these sets, but there are clear distinctions in these relationships. Journal publishers must listen to these customers if they want to navigate successfully in the new and very different period of journal publishing ahead.

Karen Hunter is Senior Vice President, Elsevier Science, Inc. (e-mail: k.hunter@ elsevier.com).

[Haworth co-indexing entry note]: "Setting Journal Priorities by Listening to Customers." Hunter, Karen. Co-published simultaneously in *Journal of Library Administration* (The Haworth Information Press, an imprint of The Haworth Press, Inc.) Vol. 28, No. 4, 1999, pp. 91-103; and: *Collection Development in the Electronic Environment: Shifting Priorities* (ed: Sul H. Lee) The Haworth Information Press, an imprint of The Haworth Press, Inc., 1999, pp. 91-103. Single or multiple copies of this article are available for a fee from The Haworth Document Delivery Service [1-800-342-9678, 9:00 a.m. - 5:00 p.m. (EST). E-mail address: getinfo@haworthpressinc.com].

PRIORITIES BASED ON THE NEEDS
OF AUTHORS AND EDITORS

Simply stated, without good editors and authors, there is no journal. Therefore, in assigning priorities, this group of customers comes first. This has traditionally been the case for journal publishers. Indeed, it could be argued that for many years we were too focused on authors and editors and not enough on the buyers and readers of the journals.

In talking with authors and editors and listening to their concerns, we see three priority areas: (1) the refereeing process; (2) visibility of the journal (including citation frequency); and (3) uses that authors can make of their own publications.

Refereeing

Two of the functions of a journal are the independent certification of the research results (peer review) and the fixing and recording of the research results at a given point in time. If one looks at the needs of authors, first priority is for fair and knowledgeable refereeing and rapid decisionmaking on acceptance or rejection. Experienced authors know the pecking order and reputation of the journals in their field and generally submit to journals where there is a reasonable chance for acceptance. In return, they want competent reviewers and the fastest possible decision. The researcher moves on to a new project and does not want or need to have the write-up of the last experiment or study stay in the limbo of the refereeing process for a protracted period. This is true whether the journal is published only in paper, in paper and electronic form or electronic only.

Younger authors in particular may also benefit from the educational aspects of the editing and reviewing process. At Elsevier Science, of those articles ultimately accepted (and the majority are rejected), about 90% are returned for additional work before they are accepted.

What is the role of the publisher in this and how can improving the refereeing process figure in its strategic objectives and priorities? At a minimum, the publisher is responsible for appointing good editors and supporting their choices for subeditors and editorial boards. The publisher must uphold its side of the equation (rapid production) so that editors do not have problems to resolve with authors ("where is my paper?") and that, indeed, rapid publication becomes a point of competitive advantage for the journal in its jockeying for authors.

Publishers must talk with their journals' editors regularly to understand their concerns and to provide needed assistance (financial, technical and ideological). Talking with the editors also helps monitor whether the editors themselves are on course, either in the process of managing the journal or in evaluating the trends to be reflected in the journal's scope. Elsevier Science has 140 scientists on staff whose responsibility it is to manage programs by, among other things, working closely with the editors of its 1,100 research journals.

One of the biggest concerns both editors and authors have is the difficulty in getting good reviewers. Niche research means relatively few people in the world are really knowledgeable about the esoteric research paper that results. Reviewing does not "count" for purposes of promotion and tenure. Regrettably, under the current system, there is relatively little a publisher can do to help in this process. We can provide systems to create databases of reviewers and to monitor their availability, performance (i.e., turnaround time on reviews) and current journal workload. We can assist with software to automate the process as much as possible. We have many letters journals with up to ten receiving stations to expedite the receipt and processing of these time-critical manuscripts. When necessary, we can fund extraordinary communication means. Indeed, in some very fast-moving fields, we have gone to the expense of starting the copy-editing process on *all* articles received, knowing that half or more of that work would be wasted when these articles were ultimately rejected. What we cannot do is get referees to return papers quickly. That is in the hands (and pleas and systems) of the editors.

With the move to electronic journals and electronic distribution of traditional journals, some people early on assumed there would be a decline in formal peer review. One well-known notion was to simply put everything on the Web and let either comments be appended (without editorial intervention) or some other market-like mechanism prevail. In fact, this model has not taken hold. Once the rhetoric cleared, the counter-voices were heard–namely, that in a Web world, if anything, more reviewing and certification by trusted sources was needed, not less.

Finally, the fact that a high proportion of papers eventually get published is often used to criticize the refereeing process. What that argument overlooks is the critical difference to both the author and the reader in *where* it is published. The editorial reputation of the journal–its brand image–remains critical, whether the journal is distributed in paper or electronic form.

Visibility of the Journal: Building Traffic to the Content

Authors are interested in having their papers read and editors want to see their journals widely disseminated. Both want frequent citations and a high impact factor. A key priority for publishers, therefore, is to increase the visibility of the journal and its articles, to build traffic to the content. In a paper world this meant selling more subscriptions, getting the journal into key abstracting and indexing services and table of contents services.

In the electronic world the publisher continues to do all of those marketing steps, but also has other options to enhance the visibility. The publisher can organize its own current awareness/table of contents services by e-mail. It can license the journals to large user communities (such as consortia), immediately increasing the desktop availability of the journal articles. This is a critically important step going forward, as one can anticipate a time that journals not available electronically on the desktop will not be used at all.

Author Rights and Copyright

In dealing with the needs of authors it must be a priority for publishers to listen to what authors want to do with their papers and to be as responsive as possible to those desires. Authors and their institutions want to be able to use their papers within their own teaching environment. Authors want to share their work with their colleagues. They also want to be able to reuse parts of their work in other publications. Publishers should be comfortable with authors doing these things.

The broader questions are: (1) does public posting of papers to Web sites endanger the publications process and (2) what is to be gained or lost by authors retaining copyright in their articles?

The question of Web posting has two aspects. First, if the paper is posted prior to peer review and acceptance, is that prior publication and, if so, will it disqualify the paper for consideration by the journal? (The same question arises with respect to universities maintaining theses and dissertations on public Web servers.) There is no black and white answer. Some journal editors will disqualify a paper distributed as a preprint; others will not. In general, this is a function of the field (the extremes being high-energy physics' rush to preprints vs. *The New England Journal of Medicine*'s absolute prohibition of any prior release of papers). Each journal (and publisher) must formulate a policy in this area.

The broader question of copyright transfer regularly raises its head. Publishers need a clear set of rights to enable them to carry out the publishing process on a realistic basis. The author also needs for the publisher to have the rights necessary to both disseminate the article and to authorize others to use it in appropriate ways. Copyright exists in the article at the time it is written (unless the authors are federal government employees). The question is, therefore, what rights go to the publisher and how high a priority does either the publisher or the author (or his or her employer) place on this process?

Journal publishers today at a minimum must have the right to: (i) publish in paper and electronic form; (ii) index and authorize others to index the work and use the abstract; (iii) copy and authorize others to photocopy or otherwise distribute copies of the work [3] and give permission for the use of parts of the work (e.g., figures, tables) by others; and (iv) adapt the work (specifically for enhanced electronic access or distribution in various collections). These are legal rights that are a necessary part of today's scholarly publication process and that of the near and foreseeable future. Without these rights, few if any publishers would agree to invest in a work. (We cannot, for example, publish an article in paper and omit it from the electronic version.)

There is another set of rights within copyright that has less to do with legal requirements and more to do with business practice. These are the broader control over reproduction and distribution. As indicated above, publishers need to consider carefully which of these they need to preserve to themselves and which can be shared with authors. Will the posting of an article–in its final published form–on a Web server interfere with the sale of the article via the publisher? Does it make a difference if the Web site is the author's home page or an organized central repository (such as the Los Alamos servers)? The publisher's answers to these questions govern whether it is essential to get a transfer of copyright and, as part of that transfer, what rights the author has. This certainly is a priority policy decision for most journal publishers.

One cannot leave the topic of copyright transfer without noting the difficulty that some people are now experiencing when trying to determine with whom to clear rights on older material. Is the author still alive? Where is the author? Those involved in this process have seriously cautioned against any movement to vest copyright with academic authors, feeling that it will create enormous administrative burdens. This is particularly true as publishers become more and more organized in handling rights clearances on a timely basis.

Publishers' priorities, therefore, in response to its authors and editors are to be as professional and efficient as possible, to be as supportive of the editing and reviewing process and to ask its authors and its editors regularly: "What can we do better?" Priorities include working for the greatest visibility and use of the journal's articles and providing for permanent archiving (as described below), within the framework of a proper assignment of rights.

PRIORITIES BASED ON THE NEEDS OF THE PURCHASERS

Assuming the content is now in order, the priorities of the publisher must also be set by the needs of those who purchase the journals. While for some journals this includes society members and individuals, for most purposes this is the library. What priorities are journal publishers facing with this customer community?

While research libraries have many needs, those we hear most often (assuming the product is a quality product) are for: (1) realistic and predictable pricing in both the paper and electronic worlds; (2) for electronic products, sufficient flexibility in product offerings to tailor purchases to local needs; (3) clearly defined licenses that conform to library principles and procedures; and (4) long-term archival access. These then should define the publisher's priorities.

Pricing

For years the pricing of journals has been the sorest point in the relationship between journal publishers and librarians. The story of the "serials crisis" is now well known and does not merit repetition here. It is fair to say that the librarians were very vocal in making their position–their needs–known. For a variety of reasons, publishers were not as responsive to those needs as librarians would have liked. And in not giving priority to trying to solve that problem, publishers lost customers. Journal subscriptions were cancelled. There is certainly more than one side to this story, but the net result remains: fewer subscriptions, lower visibility for the journal and its authors.

This coincided with the increased investments in electronic publishing. Virtually all publishers, including Elsevier Science, accepted lower profits as a way of paying for these investments. It was clear that prices could not be raised further to cover the electronic investments. At the same time, however, the products being created were felt to have additional value for the purchaser and user. The question to the publisher: can you charge for this additional value and, if so, how much? The answer is: not much, no matter how great the added value. We are dealing with purchasers who have little discretionary income. There is only so much money to go around.

The priority for the journal publisher is to work with the purchaser–the library or library consortium–to maximize the value delivered for the money available and committed. This is easier in an electronic world, because of the different characteristics of distribution and use and because it is possible to break the mold and think in non-traditional ways. The goal should also be to have predictable prices–not prices that have potentially extreme fluctuation from year to year (due to currency exchange rate fluctuations). Publishers can make this happen and that should be a priority.

Product Flexibility

Libraries in the paper world buy journals on a title-by-title basis, providing the flexibility to tailor collections to local needs. The same option should ideally be available in an electronic world. Because of the network possibilities of electronic delivery (removing the need for multiple copies), there are transitional steps some publishers need to go through to make this flexibility happen. That should remain a priority.

In addition, in an electronic world (unlike with paper) the publisher has the possibility to offer a variety of products to match a variety of market needs. It is possible to offer a very simple product (articles in PDF with only search-able bibliographic header records). It is also possible to offer a sophisticated service tailored either to a broad institutional audience or the community characteristics of a specific discipline. At the highest end, products can be customized to the individual.

The benefit of such versioning or product differentiation is that it should also be possible to offer products at a range of prices, as one part of the method of remedying the pricing problems of the paper past. In this process, input from purchasers (whether institutions or individuals) is essential. That is a priority. Just as Japanese car manufacturers are known for talking with customers to understand what features they want and are of value to them, publishers must do the same.[4]

Pricing is of sufficient concern to both publishers and libraries that Elsevi-er Science has been participating since 1997 in an experiment (known as PEAK) designed and managed by the University of Michigan. Michigan hosts the Elsevier Science journals on its site and provides access to eleven other institutions, including large and small academic institutions and corpo-rate libraries. The participating libraries were each assigned to one of three groups of pricing options and were then given choices within those options. The experiment includes the opportunity to buy prepaid, non-refundable bundles of "tokens" to be used to purchase articles from across the entire database. This has proven to be an interesting option for those who have chosen it. The experiment will end in mid-1999 and the result published at a later date.

Licensing

In a paper world the purchaser takes physical possession of a copy of the work. Under the "first sale" doctrine, that specific physical copy is owned by the purchaser. The purchaser has certain rights as to that specific copy–it can be loaned, given away, sold or otherwise disposed of. This makes sense because the physical copy is no longer in the possession of the seller.

When information transfer moved from taking physical possession of a copy to accessing bits stored on a remote server, the "first sale" notion no longer applied, as there was not a unique copy changing hands. A different set of rules was needed and publishers moved to licenses as a means of defining the terms and conditions of use.. The physical transfer that underlies "first sale" doesn't happen for digital objects, for which copies and originals are identical and which can be possessed by "seller" and "buyer" simultaneously.

An argument has been made by some copyright lawyers who oppose licensing that the first sale doctrine should still apply in an electronic environment if the original copy is deleted from the original computer when the digital copy is given (or sold or loaned) to someone else. Publishers have not publicly debated this question, but one would expect there to be a significant concern about how one would ever know if the original was deleted and the fact that the new owner of the copy would not have any contractual relationship with the rightsholder and, therefore, not be subject to the terms and conditions of the original transaction.

Licenses have been used for more than two decades, first by online hosts and then by software publishers, so it was natural that journals being offered on the Web should follow in this way. Licenses were also chosen because of the ease with which the electronic information could be duplicated and sent quickly around the world. This makes every Internet Web user a potential user of a work sitting on a Web server. In the absence of an agreement on who is permitted to have access and what they can do with the information, publishers legitimately fear serious erosion in their market if use were not subject to some limitations (i.e., the terms of the license).

As publishers and librarians gained more experience with licenses, the negotiation process has become easier. More terms and conditions are standardized and there is more understanding of the thinking on both sides. That does not mean there is agreement on all issues, by any means. Some argue that certain fair use rights are compromised by licenses. Others argue that access rights can in fact be increased under contract.

Interlibrary loan is one such frequently-cited library concern. Most publishers do not permit interlibrary loan from their electronic files. The few that do require a level of reporting that is not required in the paper world. Librarians object to this reporting. Some voice administrative concerns (there are no systems in place to gather this data–an argument for which I have some sympathy). Others argue that it is not in conformity with the CONTU guidelines, which is not a valid response, as CONTU is explicitly about photocopying and does not apply to digital ILL. Finally, others argue that to provide data on to whom they give ILL copies is a violation of privacy rules; this objection can be dealt with by creating constructs that preserve privacy.

The point here is not digital ILL but that licenses, while easier to negotiate than in the past, still have a range of thorny issues, some of which are related to strongly-held principles. In making ease of licensing a priority, publishers have to constantly listen to what the concerns are of the libraries and adapt when possible. If it is not possible, then publishers must be able to make their position clearly understood.

Permanent Archiving

Creation, maintenance and access to permanent archives must be a priority for all industry participants, as it is essential that the cultural record be permanently retained. As more and more of this record is digital, there will be an increasing differentiation between the paper and electronic versions. The electronic versions will have non-printable objects (executable software, animation, large data sets, audio, video, active links). For the moment, print is still viewed by most publishers as the definitive version, but that can be expected to change. Within five years the digital version will often be the definitive edition and the print, when it exists at all, will be simply an alternate edition.

In defining the problem, it is not enough to discuss who–publisher, librarian or other–will be responsible for maintaining the archive of record. For journal publishers there is also an understanding needed with authors as to who is responsible for the non-printable objects currently located on authors' sites. In many cases it will be the author, and that material will likely never be part of the permanent archive. If the publisher is to be responsible, this will have to occur in some formal way that, by and large, is not taking place today. The role of the publisher in assuring permanent archiving for the author's work must be made clear to all.

There has been a good deal of talk about archiving, but as yet little resolution. That is not surprising, as it is understood by all that the process of migrating information as technology changes is expensive. In addition, rights-holders have been reluctant to give wide access to any central digital archives, further reducing the incentive to invest in such an undertaking. A number of publishers (including the American Physical Society, the American Institute of Physics and Elsevier Science) have said that they will maintain the electronic archives of their journals. But, particularly when a commercial publisher is involved, this does not seem to solve the libraries' concern about the permanence and accessibility of archived material. What if Elsevier Science is sold or divided up tomorrow? Will the new owner(s) share our commitment?

One answer might be in the archival efforts of independent third parties. For example, OCLC has made permanent archiving a guarantee for the journals it hosts on its site. As a library membership organization, this has an appeal for some publishers and certainly for many libraries. Another approach is that used by JSTOR, the not-for-profit start-up seeded by the Mellon Foundation. JSTOR is creating electronic archives (from vol. 1, no. 1) of selected journals, starting in the social sciences. Publishers need to evaluate these (and other) alternatives and make decisions about partnering with these companies.

For publishers acting independently, all that can be done is to ensure that their own material is archived, participate in discussion and standards efforts and wait to see what develops with customers. But that is still a large task and must remain a priority.

PRIORITIES BASED ON THE NEEDS OF READERS AND USERS

As indicated in talking about author needs, one priority is to drive the use of the journals. That means understanding how our readers (in paper) and users (in electronic form) want to receive information and how they want to use it.

What we hear, when we listen to our customers, is that they want access to be as easy as possible. Therefore, electronic delivery to the desktop is ideal. They want to have the information linked with the other tools they use (such as abstracting and indexing services, but also things like GenBank and the full text of related articles). They also want their information sources to be as complete as possible with respect to the literature that is core in their discipline.

Another notion that has taken hold is that of the "service provider." This electronic creation brings together many types of information in a single spot: news, classified job listings, primary journals, books, secondary services, links to other evaluated Web sites, merchandise (such as lab supplies or books), etc. We have been running three such services (BioMedNet, Chem-Web and Ei Village) and are starting new ones (such as Computer Village). The response from the user has been very, very good–BioMedNet, as of January, 1999, had 310,000 members and was growing at 16,000 per month.

Not all publishers can do such community services. Societies have been in this business for decades and are naturals to transfer this role to the Web. For commercial publishers it is not so easy, as they have never had the same links to a large society membership.

Journal publishers' priorities as to satisfying their readers and users must be determined by repeated, close contact. Some of the needs can be met through products sold to the libraries. Others will be met by products offered directly to the individual, perhaps for free.

It is important to recognize that setting priorities for meeting user needs will mean careful analysis of how the new information offerings are actually used. In a paper world neither the publisher nor the library has good information on what is used and in what way. With electronic systems we have far more information available. Privacy protection means that in most cases we will not know specifically who is using the files. While publishers do not know the identity of the user, it would be helpful to be able to analyze types of use by category of user (undergraduate, graduate, faculty, government or corporate researcher, etc.) and by discipline. Where this is not readily available from the data gathered during normal transactions (as it usually will not be), periodic voluntary surveys must be substituted as a way of getting more insight into what people are doing–and what they would like to do. Electronic delivery requires that publishers give more priority to ongoing market research about their customers.

PRIORITIES BASED ON THE NEEDS OF OWNERS

When reading this heading, one may think I am talking about corporate owners and making profits. And that is partially true. But I am also referring to societies as owners of journals or other research institutions. In the end, the owner has a very strong say in what happens to the journals over the long term.

Consider what I have termed the second phase of journal publishing (about 1945 to 1995). During the first half or more of this period, as science expanded internationally, U.S. societies were largely focused on their own large membership and market. That was their priority and it was reflected in the dominance of U.S. authors in their journals. That led to conservative behavior as to the recognition of new disciplinary twigs and left the market open to international commercial publishers who did not have these constraints. We and other commercial publishers took a lot of risks in invest-ing in new journals in new fields–often taking five to seven years to reach breakeven, if then–but many now-important journals resulted. Knowing what you know now, if you had been a strategic planner within one of these large societies thirty years ago, would you have made different choices about your publication program?

Within the normal for-profit business environment, it is clear that owners–the companies and the stockholders that own the companies–expect and deserve a return on their investment. This is all too often discounted by those working in the non-profit sector as something dirty or distasteful. I recall talking with a librarian not too long ago who headed the library of a profes-sional school. She said that she made it a point when interviewing librarians for openings to note that the students in that school were there to learn how to make money. As she said she told the candidates, "If that bothers you, you shouldn't come to work here." Profits are not bad. Profits are what fund innovation and permit growth in the economy. Publishers should not have to apologize for making a profit.

Having said that, setting priorities means balancing the demands of the owner–whether a parent company looking for profits and a good picture for the stock markets or a society counting on the revenues from the journals to underwrite the member services program–with what is good for the editors and authors. The editors and authors want their output distributed as widely and inexpensively as possible. The owners want a good product, but they also want income. The publisher has to find a way to balance these two potentially contradictory "customer" needs.

IN CONCLUSION

Journals are at a fundamental turning point. While the basic functions of journals–certification, fixation in time, immediate communication, long-term archiving–remain, the electronic environment puts pressure on all of these to adapt to the new medium and to the culture it reflects. Publishers must set strategic priorities and stay focused on the targets. They can best do this by listening to their customers–authors and editors, purchasers, readers and users, and owners. All of these must be satisfied, even when their needs conflict, if the journals and the journal publisher are to continue successfully into the future.

NOTES

1. See Emily R. Mobley, "Ruminations on the Sci-Tech Serials Crisis," *Issues in Science and Technology Librarianship*, Fall, 1998. For a more wide-ranging discussion, see Brian L. Hawkins and Patricia Battin, eds. *The Mirage of Continuity: Reconfiguring Academic Resources for the 21st Century*, Washington, D.C.: Council on Library and Information Resources and Association of American Universities, 1998.

2. In an article in *Against the Grain* (in press, scheduled for vol. 11, no.1, February 1999), I describe journal phases in this way: "The first [phase of journal publishing] was 280 years, from 1665 to 1945. The first journals were published in England and France in 1665 by scholars and scholarly societies. In the subsequent years there was relatively little involvement of either commercial publishers or libraries. Yes, academic libraries acquired journals and made them available to their communities (and complained early in this century about the extraordinary growth in the literature), but libraries were not the critical market they were to become for publishers.

"After . . . World War II . . . we entered the second phase. The internationalization particularly of scientific and technical research led to the switch to English as a common publication language. Certain publishers in Europe saw this first (e.g., the Czech-in-English-clothing, Robert Maxwell). Most American societies, still the dominant American journal publishers, had a large enough community of authors and readers within their national boundary not to move so rapidly to internationalize.

"At the same time, particularly post-Sputnik (1957), campuses expanded and cloned rapidly, with new branches and enhanced facilities in the 1960s and early 1970s. There were new libraries on these campuses, eager to build science and technology collections (as well as buy in other areas). Scientific disciplines were, at the same time, doing their own "branching," with the well-known "twigging" phenomenon. Each new disciplinary offshoot developed its own societies and journals.

"This was the incredible growth period for journals and journal publishers. While it was clear that it could not go on forever, the speed of the decline was unanticipated. One can argue about the beginning of the end, but financially it was over by the early-to-mid 1980s and the Web drove the technological stake in the heart of the present era by 1995. If we want to round off to the millennium, the second phase of journal publishing was still less than 20% of the length of the first."

3. The recent case pitting three magazine authors against the Dialog UnCover Corporation makes clear that without an explicit transfer of the right to authorize the

distribution of copies (which is inherent in the copyright), a publisher cannot permit others to photocopy and distribute copies of individual articles. That means all those seeking non-fair use copies of articles would have to get permission from the author.

4. A discussion of versioning can be found in Chapter 3 of Carl Shapiro and Hal R. Varian, *Information Rules: A Strategic Guide to the Network Economy*, Boston: Harvard Business School Press, 1999.

How Booksellers Are Employing Electronic Innovations to Enhance Collection Development Procedures

John J. Walsdorf

The history of booksellers' use of electronic technology starts in the 1960s, with the founding of the Richard Abel Company and his use of computer-assisted approval selling. Prior to the 1960s, as pointed out by Martin Warzala in his *Library Trends* article, "The Evolution of Approval Services," the gathering plans "supporting efficient acquisitions of current library materials have their roots in blanket order plans of the late 1940s. Individual arrangements were made by large domestic public and select academic libraries with publishers and book dealers. In general," Warzala continued, "blanket orders operate by a library requesting a publisher or dealer to supply one copy of every title of a publisher's output or one copy of all of a publisher's output in selected subject areas as they are published."[1]

These gathering or blanket order plans were not dependent on technology, and the library was expected to keep whatever books it was sent. But some sixty-five years prior to this (remember we are talking of the late 1940s when the first gathering plans really took hold, and approximately fifteen years before Abel would start his first approval plans), there were the first American book approval plans, started in the 1890s.

The concept was the same as we know it today, and one of the fathers of the first American book approval plan was none other than Elbert Hubbard, author of what some tout as the most published book ever, excluding the Bible, *A Message to Garcia*. Elbert Hubbard first learned the value of sending items through the mail, "On Approval," or "On Suspicion" in the 1880s,

---

John J. Walsdorf is Vice President, Library Relations, Blackwell's Book Services.

[Haworth co-indexing entry note]: "How Booksellers Are Employing Electronic Innovations to Enhance Collection Development Procedures." Walsdorf, John J. Co-published simultaneously in *Journal of Library Administration* (The Haworth Information Press, an imprint of The Haworth Press, Inc.) Vol. 28, No. 4, 1999, pp. 105-117; and: *Collection Development in the Electronic Environment: Shifting Priorities* (ed: Sul H. Lee) The Haworth Information Press, an imprint of The Haworth Press, Inc., 1999, pp. 105-117. Single or multiple copies of this article are available for a fee from The Haworth Document Delivery Service [1-800-342-9678, 9:00 a.m. - 5:00 p.m. (EST). E-mail address: getinfo@haworthpressinc. com].

while vice-president of the Larkin Soap Company of Buffalo, New York. It was also Hubbard who said that "This will never be a civilized country until we expend more money for books than we do for chewing gum." (I'm happy to report that, as a country, we are in good shape by Hubbard's standards, for in 1995 we consumers spent $9.5 billion on books, and only $2.3 billion on gum.)

Hubbard was so successful as a soap marketer that he sold his stock in the Larkin Company before he turned forty, and retired to the village of East Aurora, New York, where he founded his now famous Roycroft Press, after first visiting England and being influenced by William Morris and his success with the Kelmscott Press. It was in East Aurora in 1895 that Hubbard began to apply what he has learned about selling soap to the selling of books. By 1897 he wrote a prospective buyer this letter: "I sent you for inspection a copy of a very peculiar book that I want you to see before the edition is exhausted . . . If not wanted simply return it by express collect at your convenience. . . ."[2] This sounds an awful lot like approval bookselling in the 1990s, including the warning about the edition becoming exhausted!

H. William Axford pointed out in his historical overview of approval plans that Richard Abel "made three important observations, which in turn produced one landmark conclusion. First, it was evident that in most research libraries [in the early 1960s], and in those aspiring to that status, book budgets were increasing at a significantly faster rate than personnel budgets . . . Second, there was an identifiable group of publishers in North America that accounted for the vast preponderance of English language scholarship [and] . . . Third, the emergence of a second generation of computers . . . could play an important role in the collection development in the nation's research libraries. The conclusion that Abel drew from these observations pointed toward a new and unique relationship between the academic library and the purveyor of scholarly books."[3]

Axford further noted that what Abel envisioned was "a partnership that could exploit the potential of a rapidly developing computer technology to achieve the time-honored goal of timely, comprehensive, balanced, and systematic collection development."[4]

The need for and benefits of computers, along with a large staff of book buyers and profilers, were clear to booksellers in the 1960s. As Jennifer S. Cargill and Brian Alley pointed out in their book *Practical Approval Plan Management,* "Many librarians turned to approval plans . . . in an attempt to maintain current purchasing on as economical a basis as possible. Today, with . . . decreasing budgets, librarians are again devoting considerable attention to the subject of collection development . . . As personnel budgets are being cut back or frozen, the demand for more efficient acquisitions techniques is increasing. Libraries under pressure to trim budgets and cut costs simply cannot afford to return to the expensive evaluation techniques of the past."[5] This quote, from 1979, some twenty years ago, is yet another example of the old adage, the more things change, the more they stay the same.

At the time that I was beginning to prepare this paper, I came across an article in *The Chronicle of Higher Education* with the heading: "On E-Mail List, 'Leading Thinkers' Nominate the Top Inventions." The article stated that "clocks, batteries, and birth-control pills are among dozens of innovations nominated by scientists and scholars as the most important inventions of the past 2,000 years."[6] Intrigued, I, ever the computer nerd, decided to check the story out. (After all, I received an e-mail message from the dean of a major library in reaction to the announcement that I would be appearing at the Oklahoma Conference which read: "Oh my gawd. You are speaking on electronic innovations? At the Oklahoma Conference? This is the person who used to like manual typewriters?") I went to *http://www.edge.org*, a Web site run by the New York writer and literary agent John Brockman. Along with the aforementioned clocks, batteries and birth-control pills, I also found mention of hay, Christianity and Islam, the telescope, the theory of evolution by natural selection, invention of the scientific method and the moveable-type printing press. But, strange, as it may seem, I did not find the computer listed. Christopher G. Langton, a computer scientist, wrote: "I would have nominated the computer, but I think that, although it has profoundly affected our daily routine, it has not yet profoundly affected our world view."[7]

As I sit in my home office, before my forty-five year old manual Smith-Corona typewriter (which I have trouble finding ribbons for), I am a bit surprised at this lack of status for computers, at least in this ranking of "Top Innovations." It was nearly forty years ago that William J. Goode, professor of sociology at Columbia, wrote that "Among the substantive problems for *intellectual* exploration might be the . . . Creation and utilization of electronic equipment for locating materials and bringing them to the user . . . "[8] And Robert B. Downs, of the University of Illinois, wrote some thirty years ago: "The impact of technology on research libraries is accelerating. It is quite conceivable that libraries will eventually be linked together in an international network . . . But even before such a day of wonders dawns, libraries are using technical progress and mechanisms to improve communication . . . One result, undoubtedly, will be that every piece of literature or bit of information in any library can be made readily available to the seeker after knowledge."[9]

Finally, jumping ahead with all the speed of fast forward on a VCR, we come to January 1999, where we find these two quotes in *American Libraries*: "Why have librarians been such eager adapters of information technology? Some common answers: It improves library services, makes staff more efficient, provides greater access to resources, is psychologically uplifting, and enhances the image of librarians." The writer goes on: "After two decades (more or less, depending on the library) of listening to this mentality, I sometimes wonder what information technology is really doing to the library, and I conclude that, among other things, it is creating sameness."[10] And in another article, from the same issue of *American Libraries,* we find this: "Nobody knows for sure how much information is on the Internet, but it's certain that organizational standards, services, and tools must be developed and refined to help users access what's there if the medium is to thrive as a vital means of communication."[11]

So, the question is asked, what are vendors doing to use electronic innovations and technology to help adapt their services to meet the goals and needs of libraries? Once it was perhaps good enough for vendors to say, in effect, here is my service, here is what I can offer, make your library systems work with mine. As Rebecca Watson-Boone, the President of the Center for the Study of Information Professionals, Inc., in *Constancy and Change* points out, "Most of those who study the meaning work has for people believe that the influx of electronic technologies is behind fundamental changes in work . . . They [librarians] are clearly no longer in awe–seeing such technologies, instead, as tools for supporting traditional mediating and enabling roles. That is, librarians see this technology not as creating a new type of work, but, rather, as another means to the same end: carrying out a service ideal of productively bringing user and information together."[12] This is how, according to Watson-Boone, librarians feel about electronic technologies. But what about vendors? In order to learn how vendors feel about technology, and how they see the greater availability of electronic tools affecting the way they do business, I sent out a short survey asking representatives from Academic Book Center, Baker & Taylor Books, Blackwell's Book Services, Coutts Library Services and YBP, Inc., along with one Canadian Collection Development librarian, a former colleague of mine, a series of questions. What follows is a compilation of responses from these various sources to my seven questions.

My first question was: "In what way do you see electronic tools aiding the monographic collection development process?" From the librarian of the group, Eileen Heaslip of Okanagan University College, came this reply: "Electronic tools vary in quality of information and ease of operations. My ideal book database contains accurate book information contextualized within my library's purchasing profile, has password-protected requesting and ordering functions, and produces a record which can be downloaded to my acquisitions module in order to eliminate rekeying."[13]

Martha Whittaker, Vice President Marketing, Academic Book Center, replied: "These [electronic] tools have made it possible for our customers to browse directly through our bibliographic database in ways that would have been impossible before the electronic era. It is possible to give . . . more information about titles (reviews, book jackets, publisher blurbs, TOC) to inform their book-buying decisions. Electronic ordering, up-to-date order status information and electronic invoicing all increase the accuracy and efficiency of the acquisition process." Whittaker continues: "Management data provided to librarians in a variety of downloadable formats is in my judgement the most valuable electronic tool. The ability to analyze past purchases, to identify gaps in the collection, and to make projections based on 'what-if?' scenarios using sophisticated database management tools is a boon to collection development librarians. Most of these tasks would have been impossibly labor-intensive in paper-based systems."[14]

Dana Alessi, Director, Academic Sales and Marketing at Baker & Taylor Books, replied: "Electronic tools aid the monographic collection development process in a myriad of ways. My experience is colored by Baker & Taylor's TSII product. In one location, a librarian is able to search on a wide variety of elements, including not only basic bibliographic information, but also keywords in annotations and tables of contents. Annotations and TOC, as well as review sources and some full text reviews, give a librarian more information on which to make an informed decision." Alessi also adds that "Search capabilities on LC subject headings, LC and DDC classification, as well as academic descriptors and BISAC headings allow a librarian to determine easily where gaps in the collection may exist. Finally, such things as pagination, discounted price, and book jacket scan also assist the librarian in spending dollars wisely."[15]

From Blackwell's, a dual reply was created by Matt Nauman, Manager, Marketing and Publisher Relations, and Eric Redman, Director, Product Development. They wrote: "We decided that the best answer to this and several other questions [in the survey] is to go through library workflows and show how electronic services developed by vendors have helped customers." They then broke the workflow into seven areas, and outlined the electronic development in each:

1. "*Identification*: Vendors help selectors identify more new titles by providing online databases with sophisticated query tools and online new title announcements. Library and faculty staff don't have to sort and distribute paper announcement slips. Electronic announcements are available to all collection development staff. TOC allows selectors to cast a wider selection net.

2. *Evaluation*: Online databases provide more information. Records do not have the limitations of paper, so more information can be included–such as TOC and blurbs.

3. *Selection*: Vendor systems allow tagging–so library staff avoids paper handling. This improves efficiency of the collection development workflow. Vendor systems allow online communication between collection

development and acquisitions. Links to alternative editions help selectors request the correct edition and avoid ordering multiple editions of the same work.

4. *Acquisitions*: Links to local library systems allow acquisitions staff to load vendor supplied bibliographic and order data, thereby avoiding double keying.

5. *Receipt*: Blackwell's can supply invoice information at point of receipt via EDI, vendor supplied MARC records, or participation in OCLC's Promptcat service. Acquisitions staff save time by avoiding searching their local systems to match receipt and cataloging information with orders.

6. *Cataloging*: Blackwell's can supply full catalog records enhanced with table of contents and custom local data such as barcode numbers, fund, and location.

7. *Retrieval*: Cataloging records that have been enhanced with tables of contents support better retrieval."[16]

It should be noted here that the Blackwell's response, as with most other books vendors, makes several references to TOC in the form of online tables of content display. In a poster session presented at the SCC/MLA 25th Annual Meeting, Fort Worth, Texas, Ruth C.T. Morris and Katherine L. Mondragon of the Health Sciences Center Library-University of New Mexico commented that TOC supplied by Blackwell's: "After adjusting for the effect of year of publication, circulation status, location and call number . . . , the odds of an item being used increases by 45% if the item has TOC. TOC in book records increases in-house use by 43%. TOC in book records increases circulation by 35%."[17] Further, Ann Fiegen and Stephen Bosch of the University of Arizona report in *Outsourcing Library Technical Services Operations* by Karen A. Wilson and Marylou Colver that: "From January 1996 through May 1996, fully processed material and records with LC cataloging copy were delivered for 93.77 percent of books acquired from Blackwell [via an approval plan]. Enhanced tables of contents information was included for 80 percent of those records."[18]

Keith Schmiedl, President of Coutts Library Services, said this in answer to the question of vendors' electronic tools aiding the monographic collection development process: "The development of web sites allows for quick and easy answers for librarians with approval plans. Answering the What happened? or What if? type of questions. Profiles mounted on a vendor's site allows for easy review and changes to be made, effectively in real time, thus cutting lead time to effect profile changes." Keith Schmiedl continues: "Management information can be made available so that it can be accessed and sorted in flexible ways thus producing different views of the data and allowing individual selectors and librarians to choose the view best suited to their needs."[19]

Rick Lugg, Vice President/Library System Services at YBP, Inc., noted that: "The advent of vendor-built and vendor-supported Web databases, with their sophisticated searching software and extensive title coverage, brings title selection to the users' desktops. Through a single interface, a selector can identify a range of titles in an area of interest, and that range can often be refined by publication date, publisher, LC classification, and other variables. This can be done at the selector's instigation throughout the databases, but can also include electronic notification of new titles based on an approval plan profile."[20]

Lugg continues by noting that "In some vendor systems, such as YBP's GOBI, a selector may also 'tag' titles of interest electronically, conveying the selection decision to Acquisitions, along with fund assignment, location, and other local data. This reduces potential time lags in mail and backlogs, especially if the Acquisitions Department then places the order electronically. Some vendor systems support electronic ordering, or offer other services such as integration with the local library automation system. Overall, the vendor systems support selection and ordering, reducing keystrokes, and reduce the time needed to place an order, and the time to receive material."[21]

My second question had five parts, "Are you now supporting electronic:

- ordering
- invoicing
- claiming
- order status reporting
- approval management reports?"

The replies to all these questions from all vendors were almost universally positive. I note only the few exceptions: YBP: "Order Status Reporting: Not at this time."[22]

Blackwell's: "Claiming, Order Status Reporting and Approval Management Reports–in development."[23]

Baker & Taylor: "Invoicing: . . . we are currently supplying to a few library customers. Claiming: Via e-mail only. Approval Management Reports: Not at current time; in development with Approval replacement."[24]

My third question was: "What is your firm doing to help your customers create a more efficient collection development workflow?" and it resulted in these responses: Academic Book Center: "By making communication flow smoothly and by facilitating information sharing. Some examples:

- Management of information in electronic format makes analysis and reporting more efficient and accurate, and avoids re-keying of data

- Search-only access to the database uses the Internet to allow seamless integration of faculty input
- Browser functions like citation forwarding and context sensitive links allow multi-faceted access from the desktop
- Electronic interfaces with the library's integrated systems eliminate the need to re-key data
- Shelf-ready processing and cataloging services speed the turnaround time for getting materials to the shelves and frees library staff for more complex activities."[25]

Baker & Taylor: "Primarily, we are suggesting that customers utilize TSII. TSII allows a library the opportunity to create shopping carts, whether by bibliographer or fund; it allows the collection development librarian to select and put titles into the shopping cart, which can then be transferred with ease to the Acquisitions Department for review, processing and ordering."[26]

Keith Schmiedl's reply to the questions of vendors helping to create a more efficient collection development workflow was to give "ease and speed of access to information. Easy profile manipulation [and give] flexible management statistics and reporting. Alternate work flows for approval plans, i.e., report selections on the web and allow customers to deselect prior to shipment. Electronic transfer of MARC records for selection/purchasing purposes in order to reduce redundancy in the selection process (how often a selector sees a particular citation) and reduction/elimination of keying within the library (at least for those items for which a machine readable record has been provided)."[27]

Rick Lugg of YBP commented: "We provide support for every phase of the technical services workflow–from title identification to selection of ordering (including local data) and integration of these steps with most ILS systems. In addition, we provide cataloging records embedded with local data, electronic invoicing in a variety of formats, data to create item records in local systems, and a wide range of physical processing services."[28]

My next question: "Is your firm offering cataloging services?" resulted in a "yes" reply from all vendors. Following on, I asked: "If cataloging services are offered, can customers download catalog records electronically?" Again, mostly "yes" replies were received, with two exceptions. Academic replied: "This is a planned enhancement, but currently they cannot directly download from our system. Our customers get their records via PromptCat, Marcive, etc."[29]

Baker & Taylor replied: "At this point, we are sending the traditional diskette or tape as primary vehicles for electronic catalog records. We are successfully FTPing cataloging records to a number of libraries through our Customized Library Services group, as well [as to] a few selected firm order customers. Additionally, it is possible to download full MARC records through TSII. It is also possible to create a customized MARC record with TSII."[30]

My final two questions to the vendors had to do with "electronic" slips, as a replacement for what are sometimes called approval forms, approval slips or new title announcement forms. My first question was: "From a vendor's standpoint, what do you see as the pluses and minuses of the 'electronic' slip over the traditional paper slip/new title announcement form?"

My reason for asking this question is, perhaps, fairly obvious. At Blackwell's (and I expect at all other vendors as well) we spend large sums of money each year producing and sending out these slips. During the financial year just completed we sent out over seven million of them. All vendors would be very happy if they could move more libraries to electronic slips, but there are problems and concerns. A compilation of replies included the following pluses and minuses:

Pluses:

- Cost savings in printing, paper and postage
- Efficiency in handling by both the vendor and the library
- Ease of transfer among selection staff
- Wider distribution of information to librarians and faculty
- More timely information
- Elimination of lost forms
- Tighter ordering control
- Retrospective selection
- More complete, consistent information; meaning fewer orders lack ISBNs, subtitles or publisher information

Minuses:

- Resistance to the electronic forms
- Higher cost, because libraries will take both paper and electronic records
- Infrastructure investments with no clear revenue stream
- Needs 24 hours a day, seven days a week availability
- Concern regarding response time; effect of the Internet and need for faster servers, more capacity

My last question was: "How do you feel librarians will react to the 'electronic' slip? What do you feel will be their pluses and minuses?" Martha Whittaker: "Librarians are divided–they simultaneously love them and hate them. They like the versatility of electronic forms when it comes to activating them or forwarding information onward. Electronic forms also allow various interested parties simultaneous access to a common pool of information–something paper can't do. Nevertheless you can't carry electronic slips home to review on the bus . . . That's the major objection we hear."[31]

Dana Alessi: "It's amazing to me how many librarians feel that they have to hold a piece of paper to make an informed selection when they can get better information from an electronic slip. The lack of portability of the 'electronic' slip seems to be a major hurdle. I never knew so many librarians liked to review slips at coffeehouses, in front of the TV, or in bed."[32]

Matt Nauman and Eric Redman: "We have been led to believe that there will be resistance from staff to electronic slips. However, administrations seem to be pushing it. At the recent Collection Manager Focus Group, more than half of the . . . attendees reacted positively to e-mail notification. It may take time but it will eventually be the way slips are handled in many large plans."[33]

Keith Schmiedl: "Overall the prospect of moving selection information electronically is positively received with multiple reservations about building the infrastructure necessary to make it work. There is of course concern about how faculty will react."[34]

Rick Lugg: "YBP has offered electronic slips for nearly 7 years. Of the several hundred libraries receiving slips, all but a handful continue to request BOTH paper slips and electronic. Electronic tagging is catching on slowly–for many reasons. First, selectors spend enough time at computer screens already and don't want to spend more. Paper slips are highly portable, can be worked on at home, on the bus, at the reference desk. They can be sorted into piles: priority 1, priority 2, priority 3 for budget purposes. Paper slips can be mailed to faculty . . . Most of these same tasks can be accomplished using electronic slips–the major drawback is portability."[35]

Finally, Eileen Heaslip, our Canadian librarian, replied: "I wouldn't anticipate a huge stampede to electronic requesting . . . I think the impetus within the library will come from acquisitions librarians who can see the potential efficiencies . . . There's another stumbling block apart from librarians' attitudes . . . there's only so far one can go with electronic ordering if you're circumscribed by your local system . . . I LOVE the idea of getting away from forms; as a collections librarian, I spend far too much time distributing forms . . . There's only so much information you can cram on a form. Forms show titles in isolation, not in context with other titles. Forms show only the titles your profile has yielded, not the ones it's missed . . . If you want to use trendy terminology, paper forms are static, electronic forms are dynamic."[36]

It is clear from survey comments that all vendors are concerned with the cost of dual forms, producing both the electronic and the paper forms. Rick Lugg perhaps speaks for all vendors when, in his closing remarks, he added: "Cost of forms. Vendors at this point have borne and are bearing the costs of producing new title information in both paper and electronic format. In the main, both services are provided free of charge to the libraries. It is reasonable to explore the idea of charging for one or the other variant of the service."[37] Somewhat echoing the Lugg reaction, Matt Nauman and Eric Redman noted: "We believe the point has to be made that development of vendor systems is extremely expensive. We are being asked to treat development as a cost of doing business but this is coming at a time when library discounts are going up and publisher discounts are in decline. The future of development must involve a true vendor-library partnership with both bearing the costs."[38]

Needless to say, vendors strongly agree with Susan Flood's comments in *Guide to Managing Approval Plans* that "A library should expect to pay for these services . . . through reduced discounts or as a separate charge . . . "[39]

In closing, I would like to end on two high notes. The first came in the form of an e-mail, sent to over one hundred people, with the subject being "Cool Millions." It goes like this: "Did you hear about the bookseller who won a million dollars? When asked what he would do he replied 'I'll just keep buying and selling books until the money runs out.'" The second is a more serious and hopeful quotation, taken from a recently published book, *The Story of Libraries,* by Fred Lerner: "The functions of the librarian have always been to select the material . . . to catalog it so that those who would use it can know what is available and where it is kept; and to preserve it . . . None of these tasks will disappear with the emergence of the electronic library. Somebody will have to perform them: if not the librarian, then his replacement." Lerner then closes by adding: "The anarchy of the Internet may be daunting for the neophyte, but it differs little from the bibliographical chaos that is the result of five and a half centuries of the printing press. The same science that produced the *Anglo-American Cataloguing Rules* . . . can be applied to the World Wide Web."[40]

NOTES

1. Martin Warzala, "The Evolution of Approval Services," *Library Trends* 42, no. 3 (1994): 514.

2. Paul McKenna, *A History & Bibliography of the Roycroft Printing Shop* (New York: Tona Graphics, 1996), 65.

3. H. William Axford, "Approval Plans: An Historical Overview and an Assessment of Future Value," in *Shaping Library Collections for the 1980s* (Phoenix: Oryx Press, 1980), 20-21.

4. Ibid., 21.

5. Jennifer S. Cargill and Brian Alley, *Practical Approval Plan Management* (Phoenix: Oryx Press, 1979), 15.

6. Lisa Guernsey, "On E-Mail List, 'Leading Thinkers' Nominate the Top Inventions," *The Chronicle of Higher Education,* 45, no. 19 (1999): A28.

7. Christopher G. Langton, "The Mother of All Inventions," *Edge* (1999): 4, <http://www.feedmag.com/essay/es153.shtml>.

8. William J. Goode, "The Librarian: From Occupation To Profession?" in *Seven Questions about the Profession of Librarianship* (Chicago: The University of Chicago Press, 1962), 22.

9. Robert B. Downs, "Future Prospects of Library Acquisitions," *Library Trends* 18, no. 3 (1970): 420.

10. Bernard Vavrek, "Your Public Library Has a Web Page: So What?" American Libraries 30, no. 1 (1999): 50.

11. Ron Chepesiuk, "Organizing the Internet: The 'Core' of the Challenge," American Libraries 30, no. 1 (1999): 60.

12. Rebecca Watson-Boone, *Constancy and Change in the Worklife of Research University Librarians*, ACRL Publications in Librarianship no. 51 (Chicago: American Library Association, 1998), 119-120.

13. Eileen Heaslip, E-mail to author, 26 January 1999.

14. Martha Whittaker, E-mail to author, 17 February 1999.

15. Dana Alessi, E-mail to author, 17 February 1999.

16. Matt Nauman and Eric Redman, E-mail to author, 10 February 1999.

17. Katherine L. Mondragon and Ruth C.T. Morris, "Online Tables of Contents: Impact on Usage" (poster session presented at the SCC/MAL 25th annual meeting, Fort Worth, Texas, October 17-21, 1998).

18. Anne Fiegen and Stephen Bosch, "Vendor Preprocessing of Approval Material and Cataloging Records for the University of Arizona Library," in *Outsourcing Library Technical Services Operations* (Chicago: American Library Association, 1997), 21.

19. Keith Schmiedl, E-mail to author, 15 February 1999.

20. Rick Lugg, E-mail to author, 16 February 1999.

21. Ibid.

22. Ibid.

23. Nauman and Redman, E-mail.

24. Alessi, E-mail.

25. Whittaker, E-mail.

26. Alessi, E-mail.

27. Schmiedl, E-mail.

28. Lugg, E-mail.

29. Whittaker, E-mail.

30. Alessi, E-mail.

31. Whittaker, E-mail.

32. Alessi, E-mail.

33. Nauman and Redman, E-mail.

34. Schmiedl, E-mail.

35. Lugg, E-mail.

36. Heaslip, E-mail.
37. Lugg, E-mail.
38. Nauman and Redman, E-mail.
39. Susan Flood, ed., *Managing Approval Plans,* Association for Library Collections & Technical Services, Acquisitions Guidelines no. 11 (Chicago: American Library Association, 1998), 11.
40. Fred Lerner, *The Story of Libraries* (New York: Continuum, 1998), 211.

Index

AAU. *See* Association of American Universities (AAU)

(Richard) Abel Company, 105,106

Abstracting and indexing services, 29,100

Academic Book Center
cataloging service, 112-113
electronic technology use by, 108-109,111-112
IDEAL collection, 46
journal price increases by, 41

Academic Universe, 22

Acquisitions
collaborative, 89
reductions in, 73-74

ACRL (Association of College and Research Libraries), 72-73

Aggregators, 48

Alessi, Dana, 109,114

Allen, Barbara, 1

Allen, Barbara McFadden, 2

American Chemical Society, 46

American Institute of Physics, 99

American Library Association (ALA), 66
Library Materials Price Index Committee, 41,44

American Physical Society, 99

American Society of Microbiologists, 46

Andrew W. Mellon Foundation, 79-80,99

Approval forms, electronic slip replacements for, 113-115

Approval management reports, 111

Approval plans, 73,105-106,110, 111,115

Archiving, permanent, 87-88,98-99

ARL. *See* Association of Research Libraries

Association of American Universities (AAU), 64

Global Resources Program, 77

Association of College and Research Libraries (ACRL), 72-73

Association of Research Libraries (ARL)
1998 fall membership meeting, 65-66
members' expenditures for serials, 34n
SPARC (Scholarly Publishing and Academic Resources Coalition) of, 10-11,35n,61, 64,65,67,68,69n

Authors
faculty as, 87
as journal customers, 91,92-95

Availability, of electronic materials, 28,44-45

Axford, H. William, 106

Backfiles, 45,46

Baker & Taylor Books
cataloging service, 112-113
electronic technology use by, 108, 109,111,112
TSII service, 109,112-113,114

Beilstein, 46

Bibliographers. *See* Collection development librarians

Bibliographic utilities. *See also* OCLC
as electronic publications source, 48

Big 12+ Library Consortium, 64, 65-66,68

Billings, Harold, 78-79

Blackwell's Book Services
Electronic Journal Navigator, 47-48
electronic technology use by, 108, 109-110,111,114,115
vendors associated with, 47-48

Blanket order plans, 105